C000175634

Berlitz

COPENHAGEN

POCKET GUIDE

Walking Eye
mobile app

Discover the world's best destinations with the Insight Guides Walking Eye app, available to download for free in the App Store and Google Play.

The container app provides easy access to fantastic free content on events and activities taking place in your current location or chosen destination, with the possibility of booking, as well as the regularly-updated Insight Guides travel blog: Inspire Me. In addition, you can purchase curated, premium destination guides through the app, which feature local highlights, hotel, bar, restaurant and shopping listings, an A to Z of practical information and more. Or purchase and download Insight Guides eBooks straight to your device.

TOP 10 ATTRACTIONS

CHRISTIANSBORG
See the equestrian statue of Christian IX at the seat of the Danish Parliament. See page 39.

AMALIENBORG SLOT
On duty at the home of the royal family. See page 54.

TORVEHALLERNE MARKET
This glass-walled food market is filled with Danish delicacies. See page 103.

VOR FRELSERS KIRKE
Marvel at its spiralling staircase and copper-clad tower. See page 62.

NYHAVN
Copenhagen's colourful harbour, lined with bars and restaurants. See page 51.

ROSENBORG SLOT
The 17th-century palace houses the crown jewels. See page 49.

NATIONALMUSEET
Home of the famous Trundholm Sun Chariot. See page 44.

ROSKILDE
Visit Denmark's Viking heritage at this neat little town nearby. See page 78.

NY CARLSBERG GLYPTOTEK
In a distinctive building lies one of the world's foremost collections of classical art. See page 45.

TIVOLI GARDENS
The night-time illuminations are among its many attractions. See page 27.

A PERFECT DAY

9 am

Breakfast
Indulge in a typically tasty breakfast: organic fruit and bread, soured milk sprinkled with brown sugar, pale Danish cheese and cold meat, and even a Danish pastry or two.

11.30am

Little Mermaid
Tick her off your list by hopping aboard one of the 60-minute canal-boat tours, which depart from Nyhavn and sail all the way along the harbour. It's a true delight to see Copenhagen from the water, and this round trip will also give you a good awareness of where major sights are in the city.

10am

Hit the shops
Stroll along pedestrianised Strøget, peeking into shop windows and making forays into the surrounding cobbled streets. Pop into Royal Copenhagen to admire Danish-designed home furnishings, silverware and porcelain, earmarking your favourites for later purchase.

11am

Coffee
Cross Kongens Nytorv and head for the pretty painted wharf side at Nyhavn, one of the city's best people-watching places. Sit outside with a mid-morning coffee and watch the world go by.

12.30pm

Lunchtime
Time to eat again! Wander along the harbour-side towards Frederiksholms canal, taking time to appreciate the Black Diamond and the buildings of Slotsholmen, before lunching on *smørrebrød* in the highly atmospheric Kanal Caféen (reservations are a must).

IN COPENHAGEN

5pm

Dinner

Cross the harbour onto Christianshavn for a pre-dinner evening stroll around the always-interesting Christiania. You can eat at Spiseloppen, a delightfully cosy restaurant inside the Free Town; or treat yourself at one of Christianshavn's two Michelin-starred restaurants – Era Ora and the world-famous Noma (should you be lucky enough to get a table).

8pm

Opera

The stunning Opera House is on this side of the harbour – get your fix of Puccini or Bizet in a building so ultra-modern you'll hardly know whether to look at the action on stage or the architecture.

11pm

On the town

At 11pm, Copenhagen's bright young things are just beginning to head out to the city's *hyggelig* bars and clubs. The Vesterbro district is good for nightlife – its lively Kødbyen area is the coolest place to laugh, drink and dance until the early hours.

2pm

Culture fix

Spend a few hours exploring Danish history and culture, according to your interests. You're now very close to the fabulous Ny Carlsberg Glyptotek, Christiansborg and the National Museum; or a five-minute bus ride will take you to fairy-tale Rosenborg Slot, full of quirky details – look out for Queen Sophie Magdalene's lathe, Christian IV's spyhole, and a 17th-century joke chair that squirted its victims with water.

CONTENTS

INTRODUCTION

Copenhagen (København), the capital of Denmark, is a charming seaside city with captivating architecture, history, culture, quirks and cuisine. Water is everywhere – the city is located on the eastern side of Zealand, the largest of Denmark's 400-plus islands, with only a narrow body of salt-sea, the Øresund (Strait), separating it from Sweden. Around 2 million of the country's 5.75 population call Copenhagen (and its surrounding metropolitan area) home. This compact little city heads a compact nation: Denmark itself is the smallest yet most densely populated nation in northern Europe, with over six times as many people per square kilometre as neighbouring Sweden.

Denmark is the only Scandinavian country physically connected to the European mainland – the Jutland peninsula is joined to northern Germany – and it forms both a literal and metaphorical bridge between Scandinavia and the rest of the continent. Denmark shares many of the characteristics of its Nordic neighbours: liberal welfare benefits coupled with a high standard of living, and a style of government that aims at consensus. Yet the country is also more 'European' than the rest of Scandinavia, and its appeal is universal.

Danish royalty

Denmark has the oldest royal dynasty in Europe, now headed by Queen Margrethe II – the nation's first reigning queen. Her French-born husband, Prince Henrik, died in 2018.

COSMOPOLITAN CHARM

In 1167, Bishop Absalon built a coastal castle at Havn, a strategic location at the mouth of the Baltic. Over the centuries, a city grew up around it, and Copenhagen became the seat of royalty and the cultural and political centre that it is today. The green copper towers of churches, castles and cathedrals are scattered across the skyline – wander through cobbled streets and courtyards to discover the Christiansborg complex, Rosenborg Slot and the Amalienborg palaces, and a multitude of museums explaining their significance. Danes have made an art of the cosy

Canalside life along Nyhavn

coffee shop, and the city boasts a clutch of dazzling restaurants. Copenhagen is also renowned as one of Europe's jazz capitals – lively music and summer sunshine accompany shoppers as they stroll along Strøget, the world's longest pedestrianised street.

THE PEOPLE

Copenhagen's attractions are much wider than just history, culture and shopping; one of the city's great appeals is the character of the Danes themselves. The people are gregarious, loquacious and, at one and the same time, charming and sarcastic. They simply love enjoying life, especially when it comes to the combination of family, friends, food and, of course, copious amounts of alcohol. In recent times, the Danish concept of *hygge* has made its way into the British psyche. The word conveys a combination of warmth, wellbeing and intimacy that Danes incorporate into their lives as much as possible. A sense of *hygge* can be felt in every part of Copenhagen, but is more obvious, especially on public holidays and warm sunny days, in the many parks, such as Rosenborg Have and Ørstedsparken, and popular meeting places like Rådhuspladsen and Nyhavn. Nowhere is it more evident than in that world-famous crown jewel of the city, Tivoli Gardens.

FANTASY AND CULTURE

A strong sense of fantasy and colour fills the atmosphere in Copenhagen. Postmen wear bright red jackets and ride yellow bicycles, chimney sweeps pass by wearing black top hats and buses drive along with red-and-white Danish flags fluttering on both sides of the cab.

Although Copenhagen is a major capital city, it is very compact, with a well-preserved old-town area of winding streets and almost everything easily accessible by foot. Despite the fact that the reliable public transport system is superb, walking is the best way to discover this city's inestimable charms. Long before the phrase was immortalised in song by Danny Kaye, Copenhagen was known to be 'wonderful, wonderful' – a clean, green city full of culture, with a tradition of tolerance and humour.

OUT AND ABOUT

Within a very short distance of Copenhagen, and easily accessible on day trips, are three major places of interest: Roskilde, with its superb cathedral and Viking Ship Museum; Hillerød's beautiful Frederiksborg Castle; and Helsingør's Kronborg Castle, known to Shakespeare fans as Hamlet's home, Elsinore.

Sweden is just 4km (2.5 miles) away from Denmark at the narrowest point of the Øresund. The Swedish town of Helsingborg is a half-hour sail from Helsingør on one of the numerous ferries that ply the Sound. Malmø can be reached by road or rail over the Øresund Bridge in just 35 minutes.

A BRIEF HISTORY

Well before the Vikings organised themselves into an extraordinary nation of seafarers, Denmark was inhabited by hunting peoples. Prehistoric relics of all kinds – some dating back to 50,000 BC – are displayed in Copenhagen's museums. The oldest surviving costumes in Europe have been found in this area, as have various musical instruments, including more than 30 examples of the Danish lur, which emits hoarse notes that seem strangely out of keeping with the long, graceful S-shaped stem characteristic of the instrument.

VIKING AGE

The first written records of the Vikings appear around AD 800, at which time Viking raids on neighbouring European countries were becoming notorious. At their peak, these fearless warriors reached Newfoundland, rounded the North Cape, made sallies to Britain, Holland, France, Spain and the Mediterranean, and ended up as far afield as Russia, North Africa and the Middle East. Examples of their boats are on display at the Roskilde Viking Ship Museum (see page 80).

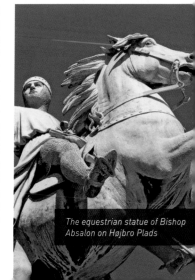

The equestrian statue of Bishop Absalon on Højbro Plads

Christian IV's Rosenborg Castle

Danish raids upon England gathered in strength during the late 10th century and the first years of the 11th century, culminating in an attempt at conquest. Canute (Knud) the Great, after meeting considerable resistance, finally became King of England in 1016. The union was to last until 1042.

Christianity had been introduced into Denmark in 826 by a Benedictine monk, and received royal approval in 961 when King Harald (Bluetooth) was converted by a monk named Poppo. A large runic stone set up by Harald at Jelling in East Jutland records that he had 'won for himself all Denmark and Norway and made the Danes Christians'.

MEDIEVAL TIMES

In 1157, Valdemar I (the Great) came to the throne. He leaned heavily on the influence of Bishop Absalon of Roskilde, and this proved a partnership of critical importance to Copenhagen, then just a little fishing village called Havn. With its fine harbour on the Strait (Øresund in Danish) – the waterway between Denmark and Sweden, which forms the main entrance to the Baltic – the village found itself well-placed on what was becoming one of the main trading routes of medieval Europe.

War hero as well as statesman, Bishop Absalon fortified Havn by constructing a castle on its small harbour island of Slotsholmen in 1167; this is now acknowledged to be the founding date of the modern city. The name Havn became Køpmannæhafn ('merchants' harbour') in 1170, and eventually København. Today, Slotsholmen lies at the heart of the city. The impressive Christiansborg parliament buildings now occupy the site, but you can see some intriguing remnants of Absalon's castle in their cellars (see page 41).

In the 12th century Denmark sorely overextended itself in all directions, and for this it paid dearly in the 13th and 14th centuries. It had interfered in the government of Schleswig and Holstein as well as troubling the growing trade of the north German Hanseatic ports. The Germans marched into Jutland. The Danish aristocracy seized the opportunity to curb the powers of its monarchy, and in 1282 King Erik V was forced to sign a Great Charter under which he would rule together with the nobles in the Council of the Danish Realm.

Nevertheless, Valdemar IV Atterdag (c.1320–75), probably the greatest of medieval Danish kings, led the country back onto a path of conquests and into new conflict with its Nordic neighbours, setting a pattern that was to last, intermittently, for centuries. Denmark's hand was greatly strengthened when Valdemar's daughter Margrete married Håkon VI, King of Norway and Sweden. After his death, Margrete succeeded through the Treaty of Kalmar in 1397 in unifying the three Nordic powers under her great-nephew Erik VII of Pomerania.

Bymuseum

For a visual account of the city's colourful past and its better-known characters, call into Københavns Museum (https://cphmuseum.kk.dk; closed until Feb 2020, when it's due to reopen in a new location at Stormgade 18).

Indomitable Margrete ruled in his name, but was struck down by the plague at the peak of her power in 1412.

During the later, true reign of Erik VII (1412–39), Copenhagen was enlarged. The city then became the official Danish capital under Christopher III of Bavaria in the 1440s; when a university was founded by Christian I in 1479, it also became the country's cultural centre. By this time, the city's population had increased to about 10,000; Schleswig-Holstein was again under Danish rule; and a castle was being built at Helsingør (the Elsinore of Shakespeare's *Hamlet*) to enforce the payment of tolls on the Øresund. Control of the Øresund was vital to Denmark's strategic strength at the crossroads of the northern seas. Dues were exacted from each ship passing through the 4km (2.5-mile) wide channel between Helsingør on Zealand and Helsingborg in Sweden.

Denmark stood in a very strong position. However, the next 200 years proved to be a turbulent period, marked by civil war, the advent of Lutheranism, and Sweden's undying enmity following the infamous 1520 'Stockholm Bloodbath', when Danish King Christian II invited Stockholm's highest-ranking citizens to a banquet, then slaughtered 82 of them in the city square. This mass

⊘ BISHOP ABSALON

Absalon (1128–1201), Bishop of Roskilde, Archbishop of Lund and founder of Copenhagen, was also a statesman, a crusader against the terrorising Wends, and a literary patron. His foster brother, Valdemar I, granted him the fishing village of Havn where Absalon built a stronghold on the site now occupied by Christiansborg (see page 39). The bishop commissioned his secretary, Saxo Grammaticus, to produce *Gesta Danorum*, an estimable history of Denmark.

Destruction of the Danish fleet during the Battle of Copenhagen

execution provoked the Swedish War of Liberation: the Kalmar Union collapsed as Sweden proclaimed its independence, although Denmark and Norway remained united.

THE REFORMATION

In the 16th century, with the unprecedented spread of ideas, the latent, deep-seated discontent regarding abuses within the Catholic Church began to be brought out into the open. In Denmark, Catholic bishops had long been putting their wealth to political and military uses, and it was left to Christian III (1534–59) to break their stranglehold. In 1536 he declared himself supreme authority of a state church based on Lutheranism, which had made deep inroads since arriving from Germany. The bishops were imprisoned until they 'consented'.

Meanwhile, the wars with Sweden lurched disastrously on. By the latter half of the 17th century Denmark had been forced to relinquish her remaining Swedish possessions, and to cede the east bank of the Øresund to Sweden. This crucial waterway was now split down the middle, jointly controlled by the two Scandinavian powers, as it still is today. As Denmark licked its many 17th-century war wounds, the city of Copenhagen had two great consolations. Firstly, the 60-year reign of larger-than-life Christian iV (1588–1648) saw a wave of new culture and fine architecture sweep the city. The 'Great

N.F.S. Grundtvig, priest, writer and pioneering educationalist

Builder' doubled the size of Copenhagen, constructing many of the beautiful Renaissance buildings that make the city so photogenic: the Round Tower, Børsen Stock Exchange, Rosenborg Castle. Then, in 1660, Copenhagen was declared a free city as an acknowledgement of its bravery during a two-year blockade by Sweden, meaning that all its residents were accorded the same privileges as nobles.

ABSOLUTE POWER

Christian IV's involvement in the Thirty Years' War and continuing conflicts with Sweden were hugely damaging. By the time of Christian's death, Denmark was bankrupt and swathes of the country had been ceded. Political and social upheavals became inevitable.

In 1660, King Frederik III matched the mood of the moment and proclaimed himself absolute monarch, thereby depriving all the nobles of the Council of the Danish Realm of the powers they had enjoyed since 1282. Frederik's absolute rule presided over a period of national unity, with a tightly controlled, well-organised central bureaucracy.

The early absolutist kings still waged several costly wars, mainly against the Swedish. Copenhagen suffered a terrible plague in 1711–12 which killed 22,000 people – nearly a third of its inhabitants – as well as two devastating fires in 1728 and 1795.

The 18th century saw major social change. Serfdom was abolished in 1788 (note the Freedom Pillar in Vesterbrogade, opposite the Central Station) and peasants threw off the yoke of the medieval landlord and began to work for themselves. This emancipation gave the Danish countryside its present character of a landscape dotted with farms, and was of enormous influence in the shaping of modern Denmark.

NAPOLEON AND THE 19TH CENTURY

Denmark found itself reluctantly involved in the revolutionary wars of late 18th-century Europe. It attracted the wrath of the British by participating in the League of Armed Neutrality, an alliance with Russia, Sweden and Prussia that was intended to prevent Great Britain from searching neutral vessels at sea. In 1801, a fleet under admirals Nelson and Parker sailed into the bay of Copenhagen. During the ensuing battle, Nelson, so legend has it, raised a telescope to his blind eye so that he could deny having seen the signal to break off the engagement.

Afraid that Napoleon would take over the Dano-Norwegian fleet, Britain subsequently demanded its instant surrender. When the Danes refused to acquiesce, Copenhagen was blockaded and in 1807 subjected to a three-day bombardment by the British Navy. Denmark had no choice but to hand over what was left of its fleet to the British, only to be forced immediately afterwards to agree to an alliance with Napoleon, who was by then marching fast into Jutland.

When Napoleon was finally brought to his knees, Denmark emerged completely isolated on account of this alliance. Norway was handed over to Sweden in 1814 in payment of war debts and the formerly vast Danish territories overseas were reduced to Greenland, Iceland, the Faroes and the Virgin Islands. Fifty years later Denmark was further reduced by the loss of the duchies of Schleswig and Holstein – a third of its home territory and two-fifths of its population – to Bismarck's Prussia. Following a spate of civil turmoil in Denmark provoked by the 1848 revolution in France, Frederik VII was forced to relinquish his absolute rule and hand over the reins of power to the National Liberal Party.

A liberal constitution was drawn up with wide suffrage, and the Danish 'Golden Age' was all set to begin. In the city, Hans Christian Andersen (1805–75), the writer from Odense, strolled the streets, reading his fairy tales to groups of admirers. Factories and housing blocks for workers sprang up, so that by the late 19th century Copenhagen was a thriving industrial centre. Meanwhile in the countryside, theologian and politician N.F.S. Grundtvig (1783–1872) established his system of popular adult high schools in 1844 to improve the peasant's lot.

THE 20TH CENTURY

In 1901 an important landmark was reached in Danish constitutional history when a government based only on a majority in the lower chamber of parliament (Folketing) was appointed. The march of the common people brought them not only into the cities and urban areas, but also right into the political struggle. In 1915, the Liberal Democrats, Social Democrats and Radical Liberals jointly forced the abolition of electoral privileges in the upper chamber and initiated a system of proportional representation for both chambers. At the same time, the vote was at last given to women and servants.

The new Danish society was put under severe strain as it struggled to maintain neutrality during World War I. After the war, north Schleswig voted itself back into Denmark, establishing the shape of today's border. Industrial unrest and economic depression between the two world wars failed to halt the progress of Denmark. In the design of consumer goods – furniture, cutlery, glass, pewter, silver and textiles – Denmark set new standards, combining utility with beauty, to the point where 'Danish design' became synonymous with good, functional, yet aesthetically pleasing articles.

Strolling in Kongens Have (the King's Garden)

When World War II broke out in 1939 the Scandinavian nations issued their declarations of neutrality. Nevertheless, on 9 April 1940 Denmark was invaded by Germany. After a token struggle, the country's defences collapsed and the nation fell under German control. However, the anti-Nazi sentiments of the vast majority of Danes were expressed by cold-shoulder treatment, and eventually acted upon through outright resistance. The Danes managed by various means to smuggle 7,000 of Denmark's 7,500 Jews out of the country and into Sweden.

The wartime king, Christian X, elected to remain in Denmark during the Nazi occupation, becoming a symbol of independence and resistance. The resistance was so organised that Denmark was already a full member of the Allied forces by the time the war came to an end in 1945. So began a new era of massive Danish reconstruction, resulting in the present modern-day society – one of the world's most successful attempts at a welfare state. Politically, Denmark abandoned neutrality when it became a member of NATO in 1949.

Economically, it was a founding member of the European Free Trade Association (EFTA), and joined the European Economic Community (subsequently the European Union) with the UK and Ireland in 1972.

MODERN DENMARK

Denmark today is one of the most prosperous countries in Europe, with its population of around 5.6 million enjoying an extremely high standard of living. However, increased immigration has challenged traditional ideas of Danish tolerance.

In the 2001 elections, the right-wing parties on a platform of anti-immigration and law and order, formed a coalition government that endured for 10 years. The country's first female prime minister, Helle Thorning-Schmidt, was elected in 2011 and faced tough political challenges, including Denmark's fraught six months holding the EU Presidency in 2012. While the aftermath of the 2008 financial crisis had put pressure on the generous provisions of Denmark's welfare state, further blows came in 2015. Two people were shot dead when an Islamist gunman attacked a Copenhagen café and synagogue; then came the refugee crisis, which stoked the anti-immigration sentiment. Helle Thorning-Schmidt and her centre-left cabinet then handed over power to a minority government led by Lars Lokke Rasmussen, head of the Liberal Party. Rasmussen resigned in 2019 following the general election in which the Social Democrats came out as winners.

Mette Frederiksen formed a new government, her popularity based on not only a tough approach to immigration, but plans to increase public spending and an aim to cut greenhouse gas emissions by 70 percent before 2030. Despite obstacles, the 'Copenhagen way of life' – green, clean, safe, stylish, and mindful of work-life balance – continues its enduring appeal.

HISTORICAL LANDMARKS

1167 King Valdemar the Great gives Bishop Absalon land by the Øresund; Absalon fortifies the fishing and trading settlement of Havn.

1254 The village of Køpmannæhafn receives a municipal charter.

1376 Absalon's castle is replaced by København Slot.

1397–1534 Denmark sets up the Kalmar Union with Norway and Sweden.

1417 Erik VII makes Copenhagen his capital.

1479 The university is founded by Christian I.

1588–1648 Christian IV enlarges the town and harbour and commissions grand Renaissance-style buildings, including Rosenborg Slot and Børsen.

1660 Copenhagen is declared a free city.

1711–12 Plague kills nearly one third of Copenhagen's inhabitants.

Early 1800s The British fleet under Nelson bombards the city for three days leaving it in ruins.

Late 1800s Denmark's 'Golden Age' of arts and science. The first railway line links Copenhagen with Roskilde.

1914–18 Denmark remains neutral during World War I.

1918 Christiansborg Palace becomes the seat of the Danish parliament.

1924 Social Democrats win power; a welfare state is established.

1940–5 Denmark is occupied by German forces.

1972 Margrethe II is crowned. Denmark joins the EEC.

2000 Øresund Bridge opens between Denmark and Sweden.

2005–6 'Muhammad drawings' in the *Jyllands-Posten* newspaper push the government into a major diplomatic crisis.

2012 Queen Margrethe's 40th jubilee. A previously unknown Hans Christian Andersen story, *The Tallow Candle*, is discovered.

2015 An Islamist gunman kills two people in separate attacks at a free speech event in a café and at a synagogue in Copenhagen.

2016 Parliament backs a controversial bill to confiscate asylum seekers' cash and valuables to cover housing and food costs.

2018 Denmark bans wearing face veils in public.

2020 A new metro line is set to open in Copenhagen to help the city achieve its low-emission goals.

View from Den Sorte Diamant (The Black Diamond building)

WHERE TO GO

You will have no problem finding your way around this delightfully compact city. Most of the important sights and museums are contained within the central section and bounded by the former medieval ramparts, so exploring Copenhagen on foot is a real pleasure. The network of canals also offers many opportunities for waterside walks and gentle excursions afloat. And if you want a change of pace from sightseeing or shopping, the abundance of leafy parks and attractive gardens provides a very welcome and pleasant retreat.

AROUND RÅDHUSPLADSEN AND VESTERBRO

Every city has a social gathering point, but Copenhagen has more than one. Without a doubt, the centrally located **Rådhuspladsen** (City Hall Square) is the most popular and, consequently, most of the suggested planned walks start from here. It is also the stopping point for the main bus routes and is near Central Station, where trains depart for the suburbs and beyond.

It is in this large open square, with its buskers and ubiquitous hot-dog stands (pølsevogn), that you can take the opportunity to observe Danish life.

CITY HALL

The dominant building in Rådhuspladsen is the

> **Museum entry**
>
> Museum opening times and charges are subject to change. It is advisable to check the listings at www.visitcopenhagen.com, www.copenhagen.com or https://cph-tourist.dk. The Copenhagen Card (see page 130) offers free or discounted entry.

Rådhuspladsen, a city-life focal point

red-brick **Rådhus ❶** (City Hall; www.kk.dk; Mon–Fri 9am–4pm, Sat 9.30am–1pm; free), with its 105m (345ft) tower. Built between 1892 and 1905, it is reached via broad steps which play host to impromptu concerts. Its main doorway is crowned by a statue of Bishop Absalon, the founder of the city, in copper and 22-carat gilt. On the roof above you'll see six bronze figures of night watchmen dating from various periods of the city's history. Each section of the Rådhus bears a different style and imprint, but they come together architecturally very much like a patchwork quilt. The main hall and banqueting room are impressive with their statuary and coats-of-arms – especially the view of the 44m (145ft) long hall from the first-floor colonnade (guided tours in English Mon–Fri 1pm, Sat 10am; tel: 33 66 25 86; www.kk.dk).

If you are feeling energetic, there are also guided tours of **City Hall Tower** and its 300 steps (Mon–Fri 11am and 2pm, Sat noon). On a clear day you can see north along the coast and across the Øresund to Sweden. In the foyer of City Hall a sign points to **Jens Olsen's World Clock** (Mon–Fri 9am–5pm, Sat 9.30am–1pm; free). This intriguing astronomical clock, said to have more than 14,000 parts, shows time around the world, the positions of the planets and the Gregorian calendar.

LURS AND LEGENDS

To your right as you leave the City Hall, on Vester Voldgade, is the unique **Lur Players** statue. Legend has it that the two men on top will sound a note on their instruments if a virgin passes by – they've been standing on the column since 1914 but have led a life of silence. On the opposite corner of the square is the dramatic copper **Bull-and-Dragon Fountain** (1923), depicting a fierce, watery battle between the two beasts. Not far away sits a bronze version of Denmark's favourite son, storyteller Hans Christian Andersen, near the boulevard that bears his name. It is on this busy road that you'll notice a very prominent feature of Danish life – the ubiquitous bicycle.

The road to the northwest of Rådhuspladsen is Vesterbrogade, which leads to Central Station, the **Copenhagen Visitor Centre** (see page 129) and Tivoli Gardens.

TIVOLI GARDENS

Across Hans Christian Andersens Boulevard from Rådhuspladsen is Copenhagen's most famous attraction, **Tivoli Gardens** ❷ (main entrance Vesterbrogade 3; www.tivoli.dk; daily early Apr–mid-Sept Sun–Thu 11am–11pm, Fri–Sat 11am–midnight; also open Halloween and Christmas – see website for hours).

Opened in 1843, this old-time pleasure park offers a joyous combination of theatrical performances, concerts, cafés and restaurants, and funfair rides and amusements, all set in beautiful gardens in the heart of the city. Visitors are welcomed

Night-time illuminations at Tivoli's pagoda

by attendants dressed in old-fashioned outfits who embody a sense of dignity and tradition – qualities that infuse Tivoli. At the Pantomime Theatre, for instance, the mimed antics of Harlequin, Columbine and the clown Pierrot are accompanied not by pre-recorded music but by a small orchestra. The Tivoli Boys' Guard brass band frequently parades through the park, dressed in red-and-white uniforms and bearskin caps. Another 19th-century tradition is the fireworks display that begins and ends the opening season.

Rollercoaster Rides & Amusements

With its lake and lawns, water features and prolific flower-beds, Tivoli fulfils its role as a traditional landscaped garden. Archaic side stalls, a traditional merry-go-round and a vintage trolleybus ride add to the feeling that you have stepped back into an older, gentler era. But it's not all coconut shies and hoopla – there are plenty of modern rides to set the pulse racing. Himmelskibet is one of the tallest carousels in the world, twirling its riders along at a height of 80m (262ft). The most extreme of the park's four rollercoasters is Dæmonen, which loops-the-loop at speeds of up to 80kph (50mph). Vertigo, one of the newest rides, simulates a flight in a fighter jet.

For kids, excitements include a Viking-ship roundabout, flying aeroplanes and miniature classic cars. For the even fainter of heart, the dragon boats on the lake have a romantic appeal. To go on any of the rides you need to either buy a unlimited ride pass (from 240kr), which lasts all day, or separate tickets (30kr–90kr).

Night-time Wonderland

As darkness falls, the atmosphere changes as thousands of multicoloured lights illuminate the park and its fairy-tale buildings, and music fills the air. The open-air stage is the focus for spectacular productions, such as *A Tivoli Fairy-tale* celebrating Hans Christian Andersen. On Friday evenings the Glassalen is the venue for pop and rock concerts featuring bands from Denmark and abroad. Jazz, blues and swing are all on the Tivoli programme. For classical music, check out the main Concert Hall, home of the Copenhagen Philharmonic (www.copenhagenphil.dk). Many of the performances are free.

Tivoli's 40 bars and restaurants are favourite meeting places for friends, families and business people, and range from cafés to top-quality restaurants. It can be difficult to get a seat on warm summer evenings, so book ahead.

Christmas at Tivoli

Tivoli throws open its doors for the festive season in the run-up to Christmas each year. The lake is frozen for skating and stalls offer tempting seasonal wares.

Thrilling rides are all part of the fun at Tivoli

VESTERBRO

Turn left out of the main Tivoli gate onto Vesterbrogade. The **Freedom Pillar** monument commemorates the end of serfdom in Denmark in 1788, and marks the start of Vesterbro, once a down-at-heel district known for its slaughterhouses and red-light area. Today it's on the up, with quirky boutiques and snug cafés. Some of the city's trendiest clubs and restaurants have moved into the former meat-packing sector **Kødbyen ❸**, making it one of the best places in town for evening entertainment – turn left down Colbjørnsensgade, then right onto Halmtorvet to find it.

No visit to Copenhagen is complete without sampling the local brew at **Carlsberg Brewery** (Gammel Carlsbergvej 11, Valby; www.visitcarlsberg.com; closed for modernisation until 2020), right on the edge of Vesterbro – either meander through the district, or hop on bus 8A or 26. The brewery's founder, Jacob Christian Jacobsen (1811–87), wanted to prove that industrial enterprises could be beautiful as well as functional, and so the whole site is surprisingly ornate. Gargoyles and lotus flowers decorate the Carlsberg chimney, while the Renaissance-style brew house is adorned with mosaics and sculptures. Jacob named his beer Carlsberg after his son, Carl (1842–1914). But father and son did not see eye to eye and Carl eventually opened his own brewery next door. You can find out more about the family – and the beer – at the Visitors' Centre.

STRØGET AND BEYOND

One of the first places you'll visit after Rådhuspladsen is Copenhagen's most famous pedestrian-only street. Known as **Strøget ❹** (pronounced stroy-et), this is a continuation of four streets – Frederiksberggade (leading off Rådhuspladsen),

⊙ THE MAN WHO MADE TIVOLI

The driving force behind Tivoli was the 19th-century polyglot entrepreneur Georg Cartensen. He had travelled widely and seen the idea in practice in cities such as Paris. His vision was to combine a pleasure garden with venues for cultural events and a fair. But first he had to persuade the king, Christian VIII, of his plan's viability. The king gave his assent 'to provide the masses with suitable entertainment and fun', and Tivoli opened its doors to the public in August 1843. Crowds flocked to the gardens to see pantomimes, shows and fireworks displays and enjoy the rides, fairground stalls and concerts. Among the first attractions was a cable-car ride. Over the years, Tivoli has been modernised and extended, but its magic is undiminished and it still retains a special place in the hearts of the Danes.

Nygade Vimmelskaftet, Amagertorv and Østergade – that wind their way for 1km (0.6 miles) to Kongens Nytorv (King's New Square). This traffic-free haven offers visitors an amazing assortment of shops, along with numerous small bars, restaurants, cafés and an abundance of street performers. Wander off Strøget to explore the small side streets: each of these has its own surprises among the numerous antiques shops, speciality stores, boutiques and fashionable restaurants.

STRØGET

The entrance to Frederiksberggade, dominated by fast-food outlets, is not exactly prepossessing; however, perseverance will bring its rewards. Where Frederiksberggade ends, Strøget opens out into two squares on either side of the street. **Gammeltorv**, to the left, is a popular place for small market stalls and is home to the **Caritas Fountain** which, dating from 1610, is the city's oldest. In a tradition going back to the golden wedding of King Christian IX and Queen Louise in 1892, imitation golden apples are made to dance on the jets of the fountain on the monarch's birthday (now 16 April). **Nytorv**, to the right, is dominated by the impressive architecture of the law courts. Each of these squares is a good place to sit at a street café and watch the procession of passing people.

The next place of note is the **Helligåndskirken** (Church of the Holy Spirit). Built in the 17th–18th century, it is set in its own small gardens. Outside is an area particularly popular with street performers and other hawkers. Just past this point, Strøget opens out again and on the left side of Amagertorv you'll see a fine example of Dutch baroque buildings – home to the group of **Royal Copenhagen** shops (see page 85). One of these, at No. 6, is the Royal Copenhagen Porcelain store, an Aladdin's cave with an elegant restaurant. It dates from 1616. Next door, Georg

Jensen (www.georgjensen.com) features tableware sets designed over the last century. For the best of Danish design, pop in to Illums Bolighus (www.illumsbolighus.com) at No. 10, an elegant department store featuring kitchenware, lighting and furniture.

As Amagertorv becomes Østergade, the shops become even more upmarket. Pause to look in the window of Halberstadt (www.halberstadt.com; No. 4) – a jeweller founded in 1846 – which features a small golden train encrusted with diamonds and gems that runs continually around.

Royal Copenhagen Porcelain

AROUND KONGENS NYTORV

Kongens Nytorv ❺, the 'King's New Square' of Christian V – dating from 1680 and still the city's largest (12 streets lead off it) – is surrounded by impressive stately buildings. The park in the centre of the square is dominated by the king himself, in the form of an elaborate equestrian statue, with four classical figures seated submissively under his horse.

On the southwest side is the Old Stage of **Det Kongelige Teater** (Danish Royal Theatre; www.kglteater.dk). It was founded in 1748, and was briefly the stage of Hans Christian Andersen at the age of 14, who tried without success to become a ballet dancer. This venerable old building, the spiritual home of Denmark's national ballet, opera and theatre,

Kongens Nytorv, with the statue of Christian V

has now relinquished many of its performances to two new state-of-the-art buildings: the Royal Danish Playhouse (Skuespilhuset) at Skt Annæ Plads; and, facing it across the water, the Opera House (Operan; see page 64).

Next to the theatre stands **Charlottenborg Slot**, the oldest building on the square. It was built as a royal palace in 1683 in the style of Dutch baroque and, since 1754, has been the home of the Royal Danish Academy of Fine Arts. Enter through the front gate and at the rear is **Kunsthal Charlottenborg**, which exhibits Danish and international contemporary art (www.kunsthalcharlottenborg.dk; Tue–Fri noon–8pm, Sat–Sun 11am–5pm; Wed after 5pm free).

Look around the square and you will notice other splendid buildings. **Thotts Palae** (Thott's Mansion), in the northeast corner, was built for the naval hero Admiral Niels Juel and is now home to the French Embassy. Not to be outdone is the wonderful facade of the **Hotel d'Angleterre** (www.dangleterre.com), one of Denmark's finest hotels.

The unusually shaped building on the corner of Nyhavn (see page 51), tucked between Store Strandstræde and Bredgade, is the beautifully preserved 1782 **Kanneworffs Hus**, which houses the jewellery shop House of Amber and a small **Amber Museum** (www.houseofamber.com; daily May–Sept 9am–7.30pm, Oct–Apr 10am–5.30pm). Diagonally across the square is the imposing seven-storey **Magasin du Nord** (www.magasin.dk), with its impressive ornate facade. This was Scandinavia's first department store and is still its largest.

SOUTH OF STRØGET

Leave Kongens Nytorv by Vingårdsstræde at the southwest corner of Magasin du Nord. You'll find yourself in an area of jazz clubs, small bars and artists' hang-outs. At its junction with Admiralgade is the massive 70m (230ft) tall copper spire of **Skt Nicolai Kirke** (St Nicholas Church). Destroyed several times by fire and rebuilt as recently as 1917, it houses the Copenhagen Contemporary Art Centre, **Nikolaj Kunsthal** (www.nikolajkunsthal.dk; Tue–Fri noon–6pm, Sat–Sun 11am–5pm; Wed free), which has a small permanent collection and an innovative programme of temporary exhibitions. At the south end of Admiralgade is **Holmens Kirke** (www.holmens kirke.dk; Mon, Wed, Fri–Sat 10am–4pm, Tue, Thu 10am–3.30pm, Sun noon–4pm; free). The church is in the Venetian style, but with Dutch gable ends and a small copper tower in the middle. The building was originally a 16th-century anchor forge, but was transformed in 1619 by Christian IV into a sailors' church. On the altar, reredos and pulpit there is a profusion of oak carvings by Abel Schrøder the Younger. Look for the model ship hanging from the ceiling, a tradition common

Holmens Kirke, the sailors' church

in many Danish churches. There are also free organ concerts on Wednesdays at noon.

Outside Holmens Kirke you are now by the canal, and it is impossible not to be impressed by the Christiansborg complex on the opposite bank (see page 39). Turn right up Ved Stranden and head for the Højbro bridge and the junction with Gammelstrand and Højbro Plads.

Within a short distance of here are three very different statues. The most obvious of these, on **Højbro Plads**, is the magnificent copper green **equestrian statue of Bishop Absalon** showing the warrior-priest in chain mail with axe in hand. On the corner of Gammelstrand stands the **statue of the Fiskerkone** (Fisherman's Wife), scarf on her head, shawl around her shoulders, wearing an apron and clasping a fish. Erected in 1940, she resembles the women who for centuries sold fish along the wharf. The third sculpture is less obvious; in fact, you'll have to look over the bridge to discover the submerged legend of the **'Merman with Seven Sons'**, who appeal to their human mother Agnete to return to them. It is attractively illuminated at night.

GAMMELSTRAND

Next, turn into Gammelstrand itself; the name means 'old shore' and, as this implies, it is the former edge of the city. This is one of the two principal starting points for canal-boat tours, the other being in Nyhavn (see page 51). Immediately across the canal lies a distinctive square-arched, yellow-ochre building with a classical-style frieze, looking like a national tomb: a monument to the great Danish sculptor Bertel Thorvaldsen (1770–1844; see page 41). Off to the right, on Frederiksholms Kanal, you'll be able to make out the arched entrance to the colossal Nationalmuseet (see page 44). Gammelstrand also has restaurants and bars, among which is the elegant **Krogs** seafood restaurant (http://krogs.dk).

Time now to proceed back to Rådhuspladsen, via a collection of interesting old streets. At the western end of Gammelstrand, Snaregade features some timber-framed houses. Continue into Magstræde, where the houses at numbers 17 and 19 are two of the city's oldest, dating from 1640. Next is **Vandkunsten**, a delightful little square with outdoor cafés and a pretty fountain. The name of the square means 'water artifice' and it is here that Copenhagen's first water pipes were laid. Continue across the next junction into Gåsegade, and look for the gabled houses with

A royal favourite

Holmens Kirke remains a favourite with the royal family. In 1967 Queen Margrethe was married here to the late Prince Henrik, formerly the French Count de Laborde de Monpezat.

Vandkunsten square

18th-century hoists at the top. Furniture is traditionally hauled up by these hoists, rather than being squeezed up the narrow stairwells.

On the corner of Hestemøllestræde and Lavendelstræde is a house where Mozart's widow lived with her second husband, a Danish diplomat. Here, the huge archways of Copenhagen's fourth town hall dominate; built between 1805 and 1815, it now houses the law courts. On Lavendelstræde you'll find typical Danish houses and shops from 1796, the year after the city's second great fire, and at the end of the street Vester Voldgade leads to Rådhuspladsen.

ON AND AROUND SLOTSHOLMEN

Starting at Rådhuspladsen, retrace your steps on the previous tour back to the Højbro bridge and then cross it to the small island of Slotsholmen (Castle Island) and the imposing towers of Christiansborg. Stop a little further along the canal at the highly ornamented **Børsen** ❻ (Stock Exchange), dating from the days of Christian IV. Its green copper roof is topped by a spire composed of four entwined dragons' tails. Christian IV was influenced by the booming Netherlands architecture of his day, and in 1619 commissioned two Dutch brothers to design the building. Currently it houses special events, and the Stock Exchange has since emigrated to Strøget.

CHRISTIANSBORG AND ITS MUSEUMS

Christiansborg ❼ (http://kongeligeslotte.dk) is the fifth castle or palace to have stood on this site since Absalon built his fortress in 1167: pillage, fire and rebuilding frenzies have taken their toll on the earlier ones. The second castle became the permanent seat of the king and government in 1417. The present edifice dates from the early 20th century, at which time Thorvald Jørgensen won an architectural competition for the design of a new Christiansborg palace. On 15 November 1907, King Frederik VIII laid the cornerstone that had been hewn out of the granite remains from Absalon's original castle. Above this a vast plinth was made of 7,500 boulders donated by 750 Danish boroughs, and then the palace was faced with granite slabs. Look up to see 57 granite masks of Denmark's greatest men. Covered in copper between 1937 and 1939, the roof of Christiansborg makes an imposing addition to the city's verdigris skyline.

The chapel, theatre museum, riding stables and beautifully restored **Marmorbroen** (Marble Bridge), which survived two disastrous fires in 1794 and 1884, help to give the palace a more venerable aspect than its more recent origins suggest. Today the castle (nicknamed 'Borgen', as in the name of the award-winning Danish political TV series) houses government ministries, Parliament (Folketing) and

Harbour bus

Give your feet a rest with a trip on the harbour bus, which connects the Royal Library's Black Diamond building with the Little Mermaid, stopping at Holmen, Nyhavn and the Opera House en route.

Christiansborg, seat of
the Danish Parliament

the Danish Supreme Court, as well as being the centre of a
complex of museums.

The most notable highlights of the complex include
the **Kongelige Repræsentationslokaler** (Royal Reception
Chambers; https://kongeligeslotte.dk; Apr–Oct daily 9am–
5pm, Nov–Mar Tue–Sun 10am–5pm; guided tours in English
daily 3pm, in July–Aug also at noon). One of the guide's first
anecdotes will probably be: 'Look at the roof here, held by
pillars in the shape of male statues, heads bent to take the
weight – a symbol of modern Danes paying their taxes...' You
can also visit the Reception Rooms on your own.

The chambers, on the first floor, are used by the Queen and
Prime Minister for official receptions, state banquets, and royal
audiences with foreign ambassadors. They are richly decorated
with works of art retrieved from the earlier palaces, as well as
pieces by modern Danish artists. Most impressive is the 40m

(130ft) long Great Hall hung with a series of tapestries by Bjørn Nørgaard recounting the history of Denmark. They were a 50th birthday present for Queen Margrethe II. Made by Les Gobelins in Paris, they took 10 years to complete. Other chambers include the Throne Room and the balcony overlooking Slotspladsen (Castle Square), from where monarchs are proclaimed.

In the palace basement you will find the **Ruinerne af Absalons Borg** (Ruins of Absalon's Palace; Apr–Oct daily 10am–5pm; Nov–Mar Tue–Sun 10am–5pm) from 1167, as well as remnants of more recent castles on the site. Also in the complex is the **Folketing** (Danish Parliament; www.thedanish-parliament.dk; guided tours in English every Sun at noon year round, bookings via the website; free).

Out in the vast parade ground, dominated by a copper equestrian statue of Christian IX, are the **Kongelige Stalde og Kareter** (Royal Stables; Apr–June, Aug–Oct daily 1.30–4pm, July daily 10am–5pm, Nov–Mar Tue–Sun 1.30–4pm). The stables are home to some fine driving and riding horses, which can sometimes be seen exercising in the square. On display are uniforms and royal state carriages dating from 1778.

Theatre Museum

In an elegant terrace above the stables is the **Teatermuseet** (Theatre Museum; www.teatermuseet.dk; Tue–Sun noon–4pm). The delightful little auditorium and galleries are packed with costumes, set models and other theatrical relics.

Thorvaldsens Museum

Throngs of painted people decorate the ochre facade of **Thorvaldsens Museum** ❽ (www.thorvaldsensmuseum.dk; Tue–Sun 10am–5pm; Wed free), on the Gammelstrand side of Christiansborg. The museum is dedicated to the celebrated

Danish sculptor Bertel Thorvaldsen (1770–1844) who, at the tender age of 11, was accepted into the Copenhagen Art Academy. Later he won a scholarship to Rome, where he lived and worked for more than 40 years. On his triumphant return to Denmark, he chose a young architect, Gottlieb Bindesbøll, to design a museum to house his sculptures. The result is one of Copenhagen's most distinctive buildings, both inside and out, its richly coloured walls contrasting with the pure white plaster and marble of Thorvaldsen's sculptures.

Danish War Museum

In a side street behind the Royal Stables, **Krigsmuseet** (Danish War Museum, Tøjhusgade 3; https://natmus.dk; Tue–Sun

⊙ DANISH THRILLER

Across Scandinavia, Nordic Noir has hit the big time. Although Denmark hasn't (yet) produced a popular crime writer with the stature of a Henning Mankell, Stieg Larsson or Jo Nesbø, it has made a huge impact in TV terms. From the moment detective Sarah Lund stepped into the frame in *The Killing* (*Forbrydelsen*; 2007), viewers were hooked. The equally addictive *Borgen* (2010) followed, about a politician, Birgitte Nyborg, who becomes the first female prime minister of Denmark. Then came *The Bridge* (*Broen*; 2011), which begins in suitably grisly fashion with the discovery of a bisected corpse on the Øresund Bridge, half lying in Denmark and half in Sweden... All three series went on to have two sequels each and both *The Killing* and *The Bridge* were adapted in other countries. Location tours are available with **Nordic Noir Tours** (http://nordicnoirtours.com). The tours start at 4pm Sat from Vesterport Station.

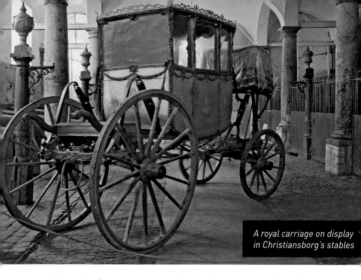

10am–5pm) holds a fascinating collection of military items, including an early 15th-century cannon from the time of Queen Margrete I and modern weapons. Cannonballs are piled high like potatoes and old military planes are suspended from the roof. The revamped Armoury Hall on the first floor houses a permanent exhibition about Denmark's bellicose past. The museum also presents the history and development of the Danish Navy.

Royal Library

Close by are the **Royal Library Gardens** (daily 6am–10pm). Designed in 1920, the gardens are a veritable oasis of peace and calm, and an ideal place to sit and rest. Although the building you see from the gardens only dates from 1906, Frederik III founded **Det Kongelige Bibliotek** (Royal Library; www.kb.dk; tours Mon 3pm) around 1653. Later it was merged with the University Library, founded in 1482. Walk around the building to the waterfront and be prepared for a huge architectural surprise. On Søren Kierkegaards Plads a seven-storey, glass, granite, concrete and steel structure appears to be leaning towards the river. This, because of its colour, is affectionately known as **Den Sorte Diamant** (The Black Diamond), and is the annexe for the Royal Library. Concerts, lectures and meetings are also held here, and there are excellent shops, restaurants and cafés. An architectural masterpiece on a very different scale is Daniel Libeskind's conversion of the Royal Boat House into the **Dansk Jødisk Museum** (Danish Jewish Museum; Proviantpassagen 6; www.jewmus. dk; June–Aug Tue–Sun 10am–5pm, Sept–May Tue–Fri 1–4pm, Sat–Sun noon–5pm). This unexpected find in the Royal Library Gardens tells the story of Denmark's Jews, their cultural heritage and daily life, through its collection of paintings, photographs, artefacts, memoirs, films and audio recordings.

From Søren Kierkegaards Plads walk across the river, along Christians Brygge, until you see the landmark building of **BLOX** on Bryghuspladsen, on the Copenhagen harbour front. Designed by the internationally-acclaimed OMA firm, it was inaugurated in 2018 and houses **Dansk Arkitektur Center** (Danish Architecture Centre; www.blox.dk; Tue, Thu–Sun 10am–6pm, Wed until 9pm) and several other institutions. The Danish Architecture Centre holds numerous exhibitions, lectures, workshops and runs a bookshop.

NATIONAL MUSEUM

From BLOX, just walk along Frederiksholms Kanal and turn left to Ny Vestergade to reach the **Nationalmuseet** ❾ (National Museum; www.natmus.dk; daily June–Sept 10am–5pm, Oct–May Tue–Sun 10am–5pm). The biggest museum in Scandinavia, it focuses on Danish history from the Stone Age to modern times. One of the most striking exhibits is the Trundholm Sun Chariot (1200 BC), dating from a period when the Danes worshipped the sun, imagining it as a disc of gold riding through the sky in a chariot behind a celestial horse. Other sections of the museum contain ethnographic exhibits from around the world (including a reconstructed Inuit camp from Greenland), classical antiquities and the Royal Coin and Medal Collection (closed for renovation at the time of writing). A hands-on Children's Museum (closes at 4.30pm) provides an interesting diversion for youngsters.

The tranquil gardens of the Royal Library

NY CARLSBERG GLYPTOTEK

From the Nationalmuseet, cross over Hans Christian Andersens Boulevard and head for the distinctive classical building with a columned portal and domed roof, which houses **Ny Carlsberg Glyptotek** ❿ (Dantes Plads 7; www. glyptoteket.com; Tue–Wed, Fri–Sun 11am–6pm, Thu until 9pm, Tue free). The Glyptotek was founded on the classical collection of Carl Jacobsen (1842–1914), a Danish brewer and art connoisseur. Under its elaborate roof lies one of the world's foremost displays of Egyptian, Greek, Roman and Etruscan art. A sub-tropical garden in the central hall appears to have been transplanted directly from ancient Rome. In contrast, the French collection – works by Gauguin, van Gogh and Monet, Rodin sculptures and a complete set of Degas bronzes – is in a glorious modern wing, built in 1996 and designed by Henning Larsen (creator of Copenhagen's Opera House).

UNIVERSITY QUARTER AND PARKS

From Rådhuspladsen, go northwest for a short way along Vester Voldgade and then turn right into narrow Studiestræde, home to a melange of antiques shops, bookstalls and boutiques gathered in an 18th-century setting.

At Studiestræde 6 a plaque records that H.C. Ørsted, who discovered electro-magnetism in 1820, lived here. A few metres further on, at the corner of Nørregade, is one of Copenhagen's oldest preserved buildings, the former Bispegården (Bishop's Residence), built in 1500 and part of the university. Nearby on Bispetorvet, a 1943 monument commemorates the 400th anniversary of the introduction of the Reformation to Denmark.

COPENHAGEN CATHEDRAL

At the end of Studiestræde stands the **Domkirke** ⓫ (Cathedral) of Copenhagen, known as **Vor Frue Kirke** (Church of Our Lady; www.koebenhavnsdomkirke.dk; Mon–Thu, Sat 8.30am–5pm, Fri 8.30–10.30am, noon–5pm, Sun noon–4.30pm; free). Bishop Absalon's successor, Sunesen, is said to have laid its foundations in the 12th century, but by 1316 it had already burned down four

A good deed

The word *mitzvah* on the door of the Danish Jewish Museum means 'a good deed'. It relates to the remarkable rescue in 1943 of 7,000 Jews who, in the face of deportation to Nazi concentration camps, were hidden and taken in small boats to Sweden.

The elaborate Glyptoteket gallery

times. Later, two further constructions were destroyed – by the great 1728 fire and by British bombardment in 1807. The present church was reconstructed by V.F.K. and C.F. Hansen between 1811 and 1829. Its austere interior is relieved by a collection of heroic statues by Bertel Thorvaldsen: 12 massive marble Apostles line the aisle, while an orange-lit altar is surrounded by bronze candelabra and dominated by his figure of Christ.

UNIVERSITY AND GRÅBRØDRETORV

Proceed along the north side of the Cathedral. On the left is the main Copenhagen University block, which dates back in its present form only as far as the 1830s. The university was founded in 1479. This is a typical student area with a number of interesting bookshops and cafés.

Turn right into Fiolstræde, a lively spot for alfresco dining, and left into Skindergade, which leads into **Gråbrødretorv** (Greyfriar's

Picturesque Gråbrødretorv

Square), a large, picturesque traffic-free square surrounded by brightly painted 18th-century houses. It was the site of a Franciscan monastery until the Reformation. Cafés and restaurants proliferate here.

ROUND TOWER

Continue along Skindergade to Købmagergade and you'll find yourself at the foot of one of Copenhagen's most beloved landmarks, the **Rundetaarn** ⑫ (Round Tower; www.rundetaarn.dk; early Apr–Sept daily 10am–8pm, Oct–early Apr Tue–Wed 10am–9pm, Thu–Mon until 6pm). The Round Tower was built by Christian IV in 1642 as part of his vision to provide an astronomical observatory, church and university library for 17th-century scholars. You can walk to the top of the 36m (118ft) high tower, but not by any ordinary means – steps would have been impractical for raising the heavy equipment needed here. Instead, a wide spiral ramp, 210m (690ft) long, winds around inside the tower. Not only did Tsar Peter the Great ride up to the top on horseback in 1716, but his empress followed him in a horse-drawn coach. You can see the core of tower looking down from a glass floor and there is a splendid view over the rooftops of the old city from the top. **Trinitatis Kirke** (Trinity Church) is to the rear of the tower; look through the glass panel in the wall at the bottom of the ramp. The library hall above is now used for exhibitions and concerts.

The building across Købmagergade from the Round Tower, at the corner with Krystalgade, is the Regensen university hostel. Although students have lived here since 1623, most of the present structure dates from the 18th century. A couple of hundred metres along Krystalgade stands the Synagogue of Copenhagen (www.mosaiske.dk), inaugurated in 1833.

ROSENBORG SLOT

Backtrack to the Round Tower and turn right, following Landemærket to its end at Copenhagen's favourite park, **Kongens Have** (King's Garden), filled with sunbathers, picnickers and families in summer. This garden was laid out in 1606–34 by Christian IV, who found Christiansborg Palace too official and oppressive. He built himself a small country mansion in a corner of the site, outside the town walls, eventually expanding it into the three-storey Dutch Renaissance-style **Rosenborg Slot** ⑬ (Rosenborg Castle; www.kongernessamling.dk; mid-Apr–May, Sept–Oct daily 10am–4pm, June–Aug 9am–5pm, Nov–mid-Apr Tue–Sun 10am–3pm). Rosenborg became home for the next three generations of kings until Frederik IV erected Frederiksberg Castle in 1710. Since 1838 it has been a royal museum of considerable grace and the home of the crown jewels.

The castle's rooms are arranged chronologically, beginning with Christian IV's tower-room study, still furnished in its original style. The Knights' Hall, with tapestries depicting Danish

Old observatory

The Rundetaarn (Round Tower) has the oldest functioning observatory in Europe. If you happen to be here in winter, you can view the night sky through its telescope (www.rundetaarn.dk; late Nov–Mar Tue–Wed 6–9pm).

A spiral ramp winds around the inside of the Round Tower

victories in the Swedish Wars, an ornate ceiling and three almost life-size silver lions, contains one of the world's largest collections of silver furniture, mostly from the 18th century.

The crown jewels are held in the treasury. In addition to the oldest existing insignia of the Order of the Elephant, there are 18 cases of crowns, gilded swords, precious stones and coronation cups – as well as silver boxes containing the umbilical cords of eight royal children. The centrepiece of this regal collection is the 17th-century crown of the absolute monarchy – made out of gold, diamonds, sapphires and garnets and weighing over 2kg (4lbs).

Also not to be missed is the nearby **David Collection ⑭** (Kronprincessegade 30; www.davidmus.dk; Tue, Thu–Sun 10am–5pm, Wed until 9pm; free), which has outstanding European and Islamic fine art collections.

On the other side of Rosenborg, across Øster Voldgade, visiting gardeners will be particularly interested in the **Botanisk Have ⑮** (Botanical Gardens; http://botanik.snm.ku.dk; daily Apr–Sept 8.30am–6pm, Oct–Mar 8.30am–4pm; free). It has Denmark's largest collection of living plants. The city's zoological, botanical and geological collections have been recently merged into one stunning new **Natural History Museum of Denmark** (http://nyt.snm.ku.dk), to be completed by 2022.

FINE ARTS MUSEUM

Art lovers should allow themselves time to explore the **Statens Museum for Kunst** ⑯ (National Gallery of Denmark; Sølvgade 48–50; www.smk.dk; Tue, Thu–Sun 10am–6pm, Wed until 8pm; free, charge for special exhibitions), just north of the Botanical Gardens. Paintings from early Dutch to modern Danish, including a large Matisse collection and perhaps the world's finest collection of Dürer prints, are housed in a light, airy and beautifully renovated building.

Across the park at Stockholmsgade 20 is **Den Hirschsprungske Samling** (Hirschsprung Collection; www. hirschsprung.dk; Wed–Sun 11am–4pm), a delightful museum packed with 19th-century Danish painting, sculpture and decorative art. Heinrich Hirschsprung, a tobacco merchant, donated the works to the state in 1902. Look out for the portraits and landscapes of C.W. Eckersberg (1783–1853), whose meticulous style had a far-reaching influence.

It's possible to return to Rådhuspladsen by bus or by train from Nørreport Station. But, if you prefer to walk, there is another surprise: the leafy **Ørsteds Parken**, on the right-hand side of Nørre Voldgade. This charming park offers a wonderful respite during daylight hours.

NYHAVN AND BEYOND

This walk begins at Kongens Nytorv (bus 26 from Rådhuspladsen). Cross the square towards **Nyhavn** ⑰; the name literally means 'new harbour' and immediately you'll notice the nautical flavour of this former 'sailors' street', once overflowing with bars and brothels. Over the centuries the two sides of the canal have developed into a remarkable illustration of old Copenhagen. At the Kongens Nytorv end of the canal, which was dug in 1671 to enlarge the harbour, stands a sizeable old anchor, a memorial to the Danish sailors killed in World War II. On either side of the canal itself, an unusual collection of vessels lies at anchor with their masts colourfully bedecked with the Danish flag. This sight, combined with numerous restaurants and bars with outside terraces, and the antiques shops and other stores on the north side, draws thousands of people who are only too happy to eat, drink and socialise in such an attractive and lively setting.

This is a street with everything – history, architecture, nightlife and a constant passage of colourful small vessels. It was even home to Hans Christian Andersen, who lived here first at number 67 from 1854–64 and later at number 18.

Walk to the end of Nyhavn on the north side (with all the cafés), and you'll pass Nyhavn 71 (www.71nyhavnhotel.com), a superb hotel conversion of an 18th-century warehouse. Just beyond is a view over the inner harbour to the Christianshavn area, where the spiralling steeple of Vor Frelsers Kirke dominates the skyline (see page 62).

Elephant order

The Order of the Elephant is Denmark's highest decoration. Instituted by Christian V in 1693, the insignia is worn by members of the royal family and can be bestowed upon foreign heads of state. Britain's Queen Elizabeth II is a member of the Order.

AMALIEHAVN GARDENS

Turn left down Toldbodgade to Skt Annæ Plads. This is a fine boulevard lined with consulates and distinguished old offices, with an equestrian statue of Christian X at the end overlooking Bredgade. To your right is the **Royal Danish Playhouse** ⓲ (Skuespilhuset; https://kglteater.dk). Cross the

Formal gardens around Rosenborg Slot

square, turn right and then left along the waterfront to the pleasant **Amaliehavn Gardens**. These were created by Belgian landscape architect Jean Delogne in 1983 using French limestone and Danish granite. The bronze pillars around the fountain were designed by Italian sculptor Arnaldo Pomodoro. Across the water you'll see the magnificent Opera House (see page 64).

AMALIENBORG PALACE

The road leading away from the water takes you to one of the most attractively symmetrical squares in Europe, **Amalienborg Plads**. A huge equestrian statue of Frederik V, 21 years in the making, dominates the centre of the square and gives you a clue that you are now in the proximity of royalty. The four (superficially) identical mansions that line the octagonal perimeter were designed by superstar 18th-century architect Nicolai Eigtved as town mansions for four noblemen. After

Christiansborg Palace was destroyed by fire in 1794, the homeless royal family purchased the mansions from their aristocratic owners, and has lived here since. Today, collectively known as **Amalienborg Slot** ⑲ (Palace), these buildings are considered to be one of the finest rococo ensembles in Europe.

Four roads converge at right angles on the courtyard, while bearskin-clad soldiers guard each of the palaces and corners, with an extra sentry posted at the gateway between the two palaces to your left. The wing to the left of the colonnade is Christian IX's Palace, the winter residence of Queen Margrethe. On the right of the colonnade, **Christian VII's Palace** (www.kongernessamling.dk) is used for receptions and to house royal guests.

Continuing around the square, the third building, Christian VIII's Palace, houses the **Amalienborg Palace Museum** (www.kongernessamling.dk; Jan–Apr Tue–Sun 10am–3pm, May, Sept–Oct daily 10am–4pm, June–Aug daily 10am–5pm, Nov–Dec Tue–Sun 11am–3pm), where the Royal Collection is on show in the splendid private apartments of the Danish Glücksburg kings. Among the exhibits are treasured works of art given to Christian IX (reigned 1863–1906) and Queen Louise by their six children, some of whom married into other leading European royal families. The fourth building is Frederik VIII's Palace, home to Crown Prince Frederik and his family. The name Amalienborg came from the wife of Frederik III, Queen Sophie Amalie.

The main attraction at Amalienborg when the Queen is in residence is the daily **Changing of the Guard**. At 11.27am the guards leave their barracks near Rosenborg Castle (see page 49) in formation, and march through the city streets so as to arrive in the palace square just before noon, moving from one sentry box to another in a series of foot-stamping ceremonies. Guardsmen march to the accompaniment of a band, their

Colourful Nyhavn

black bearskins rippling in the breeze. They wear blue trousers with white stripes and highly polished boots; on festive occasions they dress in red tunics with white shoulder straps.

CHURCHILL PARK

Leave the square via Amaliegade and follow it north for about 730m/yards to its junction with Esplanaden. Churchill Parken is on the opposite side of the road and has several interesting sights.

The **Frihedsmuseet** 20 (Museum of the Danish Resistance 1940–45; www.natmus.dk) is located at one of the prettiest spots in the city – especially in springtime when the daffodils are in bloom. In contrast, the museum provides a graphic record of wartime darkness and danger during the German occupation. Displays illustrate the daring exploits of the Resistance Movement. Due to a fire in 2013 the museum will be closed until spring 2020; check website for reopening times.

Amalienborg Plads and Palace, home of the royal family

Just beyond, the Anglican **St Alban's Church** (www.st-albans. dk) looks as if it has been transplanted from an English country village. It was indeed constructed amid the green lawns of Churchill Park in 1887 by an English architect. On a small slope next to the church there is a sight that is guaranteed to hold your attention. Copenhagen has numerous fountains but this, the **Gefion Fountain**, is the most spectacular. It was commissioned by the Carlsberg Foundation, and in 1908 sculptor Anders Bundgaard's depiction of the legend of the Nordic goddess Gefion – who turned her four sons into oxen and used them to pull the island of Zealand from Sweden – was unveiled.

THE LITTLE MERMAID

Follow the right-hand path through delightful gardens past the fountain and walk much further on to Langelinie (a water-side pier/promenade). Located just before the marina and the cruise-ship dock, near the water's edge, is Denmark's most famous statue, **Den Lille Havfrue** ㉑ (the Little Mermaid). In Andersen's fairy tale, this tragic sea-girl exchanged her voice for human legs in order to gain the love of an earthly prince, but had to watch in silence as he jilted her for a human princess. In desperation, she threw herself into the sea and turned into foam. To the dismay of both visitors and Danes, the mermaid has frequently been vandalised. Fortunately, the workshop of sculptor Edvard Eriksen retains the original moulds from 1913, and new parts can be cast if necessary. Although famous, it must be said that the statue is rather small and unassuming.

THE CITADEL

After viewing the Little Mermaid, take the road running inland from the water, cross a bridge and descend the flight of steps on the left. This leads to a wooden bridge on the far side of which is **Kastellet** ㉒ (Citadel; daily summer 6am–10pm, winter until 8pm), a star-shaped fortress with five bastions. It was begun by Frederik III in 1662. Building continued until 1725 and today the fortress is still in use by the army – the church, prison and main guardhouse having resisted the assaults of time. It is a delightfully peaceful enclave, with a charming windmill (1847) and some remains of the old ramparts well worth seeing.

Leave by the wooden bridge leading south into Churchill Parken, and then turn right onto Esplanaden. Cross Store Kongensgade into Gernersgade and you are in the heart of **Nyboder** ㉓ (New Dwellings), whose long rows of houses were first built between 1631 and 1641 by Christian IV as dwellings for his sailors. More houses were built in the 18th and 19th centuries. Painted yellow-ochre, with steep gabled roofs and shuttered windows, they form a fashionable, well-preserved community of homes still inhabited by navy personnel as well as civilians. You can see what life here used to be like at **Nyboders Mindestuer** (St Pauls Gade 24; http://nyboders-mindestuer.dk; Sun 11am–2pm), a small museum based in the cramped rooms of two 17th-century houses.

A STROLL ALONG BREDGADE

Backtrack to Bredgade and turn right. The area from here to Kongens Nytorv is a residential quarter of substantial granite houses and quadrangles. It was planned by architect Nicolai Eigtved at about the same time as Amalienborg. At number 68 you'll find **Designmuseum Danmark** (http://designmuseum. dk; Tue, Thu–Sun 10am–6pm Wed until 9pm). Housed in an

Majestic Marmorkirken (the Marble Church)

attractive rococo building (a former hospital) dating from 1757, the museum focuses on Danish and European decorative art, along with Oriental handicrafts dating from the Middle Ages to the present.

On one side of the museum, at number 70, there is a plaque commemorating the death of the philosopher Søren Kierkegaard in 1855. On the other side, at number 64, is Skt Ansgars Kirke, centre of the modest Roman Catholic community since 1842. A museum documents the history of Catholicism in the city since its virtual extinction in the Reformation of 1536. Immediately after the church stands the **Medicinsk Museion** (Bredgade 62; www.museion.ku.dk; Tue–Fri 10am–4pm, and Sat–Sun noon–4pm; guided tours in English Tue–Fri 2pm, Sat–Sun 1.30pm) – the squeamish may shy away from its fascinating collection of medical artefacts, past and present. Then it comes as a surprise to see, across the road, the golden onion-shaped domes of Alexander Nevsky Kirke, built for the Russian Orthodox community in 1883.

MARBLE CHURCH

A few steps further and the great dome of the **Marmorkirken** ❷❹ (Marble Church; www.marmorkirken.dk; Mon–Thu and Sat 10am–5pm, Fri and Sun noon–5pm; free; visits to the dome Sat–Sun 1pm, mid-June–Aug and one week in mid-Oct also Mon–Fri 1pm), officially called the Frederiks Kirken, rises high to your right. Measuring 31m (100ft) in diameter, this is one of the largest church domes in Europe. The cornerstone was laid by Frederik V in 1749. However, the Norwegian marble required for the building became so expensive that the project was halted. It was eventually completed using Danish marble and consecrated in 1894.

Inside, the dome is decorated with rich frescoes in blue, gold and green, representing the Apostles. Outside, the building is surrounded by statues of personalities of the Danish Church, including St Ansgar, who helped to bring Christianity to Denmark, and Grundtvig, the 19th-century educationalist. On the roof are 16 religious figures, from Moses to Luther. Continue along Bredgade to Kongens Nytorv past an array of boutiques, antiques shops and galleries.

CHRISTIANSHAVN AND HOLMEN

Though there's so much to see within a small radius of Rådhuspladsen and Kongens Nytorv, it's worth spending a few hours across the Knippelsbro bridge in **Christianshavn**.

All quiet at the Citadel

The area was named Christian's Harbour after Christian IV, and it looks like a slice of Amsterdam, reflecting the king's predilection for Dutch architecture.

CHRISTIANS KIRKE

Having crossed Knippel Bridge you are on Torvegade. Turn right at the intersection with Strandgade and stroll to the sombre **Christians Kirke** ㉕ (www.christians kirke.dk; Tue–Fri 10am–4pm). Built in 1755 by

Twentieth-century design icons, Designmuseum Danmark

Nicolai Eigtved, it possesses an unexpected interior layout with three tiers of galleries reminiscent of an old-time music hall. The tower was added in 1769.

Now backtrack and after crossing Torvegade continue on Strandgade until you reach Gammel Dok, the impressive former warehouse housing the Danish Art Workshops where artists can carry out their projects at special studios and workshops. The area has numerous 17th- and 18th-century houses with cobbled courtyards. N.F.S. Grundtvig spent some years at number 4B. Living at number 6 in the early 18th century was Admiral Peter Wessel Tordenskjold – a Danish-Norwegian hero who won battles at sea, but whose exuberant lifestyle ashore lost him many good neighbours. It's said that every time he called *skål* (cheers) during his frequent banquets, a salute would be fired from two cannons at the main doorway, with many a sleepless night had by all until his death in a duel in 1720.

VOR FRELSERS KIRKE

Follow Skt Annæ Gade from Strandgade towards the distinctive twisted spire of **Vor Frelsers Kirke** ㉖ (Church of Our Saviour; www.vorfrelserskirke.dk; daily 11am–3.30pm; tower open daily May–Sept Mon–Sat 9.30am–7pm, Sun from 10.30am, Oct–mid-Dec and late-Feb–Apr Mon–Sat 10am–4pm, Sun from 10.30am, closed mid-Dec–late-Feb), consecrated in 1696. Its most dominant exterior feature, the dizzying staircase that twists four times around the creaking wooden tower, was designed by Lauridz de Thurah and completed in 1752. A total of 400 steps, 150 on the outside, lead from the entrance of the church to the gilt globe and Christ figure on top of the spire.

The inside of the church has many points of interest, including its choir screen, guarded by six wooden angels; the ornate white marble font supported by four cherubs; the altar dating from 1732, replete with allegorical statues and Dresden-like figures playing in the clouds; the tinkling carillon; and in particular the monumental organ, built in 1700 and several times remodelled, most recently in 1965. Beautifully ornamented, the whole construction is supported by two large stucco elephants.

⊙ SØREN KIERKEGAARD

The top-hatted figure of Søren Kierkegaard (1813–55) was a familiar sight to Copenhageners as he took his daily walk along the city's cobbled streets. Regarded as one of the founders of Existentialism, Kierkegaard's philosophy developed out of personal anguish and his distaste for organised religion. A small exhibition devoted to Kierkegaard at Københavns Museum (Museum of Copenhagen; https://cphmuseum.kk.dk) is due to reopen in 2020 at Stormgade 18.

The grandiose Marble Church, modelled on St Peter's in Rome

CHRISTIANIA

Outside Vor Frelsers Kirke, turn left onto Prinsessegade and follow the brick wall to a somewhat more esoteric experience. In 1971, a group of local people broke into an abandoned military barracks here and founded **Christiania 27** free state. Denmark proclaimed it a social experiment soon thereafter, and it has provoked controversy ever since. For many years, soft drugs were sold from stalls on the main street, although recent political pressure and police clampdowns have stopped this open sale. Around 1,000 people live and work in this community, with its eclectic collection of eateries, oddball architecture and a great concert venue, Loppen. However, as the Free Town stands on a piece of prime real-estate in a fast-growing city, it's unlikely to survive much longer – visit while you can. To get the most out of Christiania, take a guided tour (www.rundvisergruppen.dk; Sat and Sun 3pm), run by local residents, departing from the main gate.

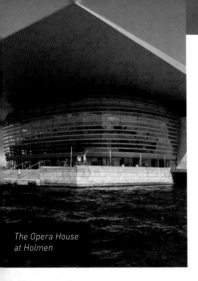

The Opera House at Holmen

OPERA HOUSE

From Christiania, continue along Prinsessegade to Holmen, where Copenhagen's dramatic modern **Opera House** 28, which opened in 2005, dominates the former docklands site on the harbour front. Designed by Danish architect Henning Larsen, the modernist Opera House is topped by a spectacular 'floating' roof. The enormous, airy foyer holds an elegant pre-show restaurant and looks like something out of *2001: A Space Odyssey*. A number of the Nordic region's most eminent artists have contributed to the interior decor, including Per Kirkeby, who created stunning bronze reliefs.

OUTLYING DISTRICTS

Although most of the main tourist attractions are clustered in and around the pretty old town, there are some gems worth seeking out in other areas of the city.

FREDERIKSBERG

The leafy suburb of Frederiksberg (technically not part of Copenhagen, although it is surrounded by the city) is a great place for families. In summer, you can hire boats and row around the meandering canal system in rolling, romantic

Frederiksberg Have (Frederiksberg Gardens; boats available May–Sept Mon–Fri 10am–5pm, Sat–Sun and hols noon–6pm). Look out for the colony of tame grey herons that wander the lawns and paths close to the Chinese pavilion (May–Sept Sun 2–4pm; free; cross by the ferry boat).

From the park, there's a good view of architect Norman Foster's famous elephant house at **Zoologisk Have** (Copenhagen Zoo; Roskildevej 32; www.zoo.dk; July–Aug daily 9am–8pm, Apr–June Mon–Fri 9am–6pm, Sat–Sun 9am–8pm, Sept daily 9am–6pm, Oct daily 9am–5pm, Nov–Mar Mon–Fri 10am–4pm, Sat–Sun 9am–4pm). The zoo has lots on offer, including tigers, brown bears, polar bears and a pride of lions. If you're in the area, it's worth paying a visit to the nearby **Glass Museum** (Cisternerne – Museet for Moderne Glaskunst;

Copenhagen rooftops from Vor Frelsers Kirke

www.cisternerne.dk; Tue–Wed, Fri–Sun 11am–6pm, Thu until 8pm, closed Dec–Feb), housed in an underground water tank: glowing glass, drips of water, and crypt-like arches lend it an almost medieval atmosphere.

Also in Frederiksberg, the **Musikmuseet ㉙** (Danish Music Museum; Rosenørns Allé 22; www.natmus.dk; Sat–Sun 10am–4pm) has a collection of 3,800 instruments displayed in a former broadcasting house.

NØRREBRO

Nørrebro is another working-class district beginning the shift towards gentrification. **Skt Hans Torv ㉚** and the surrounding streets contain some great cafés and restaurants, while interesting independent shops selling clothes and antiques are scattered along Elmegade and Ravnsborggade. It may sound odd, but one of the area's biggest attractions is **Assistens Cemetery ㉛**, where Copenhageners like to picnic, jog and play with their kids alongside the graves of famous Danes like Hans Christian Andersen, Niels Bohr and Søren Kierkegaard.

Beyond Nørrebro, in Østerbro district, a new museum of post, telecoms and communication, Enigma (Øster All 1, 2100 Copenhagen; (www.

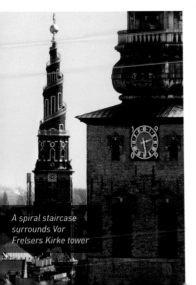

A spiral staircase surrounds Vor Frelsers Kirke tower

enigma.dk, tel: 3341 0920; Mon–Tue 11am–6pm, Sat & Sun 9am–4pm; hours vary in school holidays) will fully open in 2020. Until then, the building hosts talks, debates and workshops about Denmark's communication history. You can also buy books, games and gadgets in the store, and there's a café on site.

> ### Opera house tour
>
> Whether or not you're able to see an opera or ballet production at the city's new Opera House, a guided tour round the building is recommended – see the website https://kglteater.dk for days and times and to book tickets, or tel: 33 69 69 69. The harbour bus and bus 9A serve the site.

BISPEBJERG

A 25-minute journey from Rådhuspladsen on the number 6A bus brings you to the immense **Grundtvigs Kirke** ❷ (www.grundtvigskirke.dk; Tue–Wed, Fri–Sat 9am–4pm, Thu until 6pm, Sun noon–4pm; free) in the northwestern suburb of Bispebjerg. The church is a monument to N.F.S. Grundtvig (1783–1872), a renowned educationalist, austere parson and prolific hymnwriter. Built between 1921 and 1940, it is also a monument to early 20th-century Danish architecture. The church's design by Peder Jensen-Klint is simple but effective. Everything is in paleyellow brick, from the 50m (160ft) tower to the altar.

EXCURSIONS

In a country of 44,030 sq km (16,630 sq miles), nature has ingeniously divided Denmark into a land of more than 450 islands so that you are never more than 50km (30 miles) from the sea. Copenhagers have their own beach, woodlands and wide lake area, and it is easy to organise an excursion. Options include boat trips, windmill and water-mill sightings, a visit to a royal country castle, and the chance to explore two fabulous art galleries and a couple of pretty, traditional villages.

STORE MAGLEBY AND DRAGØR

Travellers arriving by plane will already have visited Amager island – but there are far more charming places here than the international airport. A number 350S bus from Kongens Nytorv will take you south to the village of Store Magleby and then to charming Dragør. As many of the shops in Dragør are open on Sunday in summer, this is a good day to take the trip.

In an old farmhouse on the village street in **Store Magleby** you'll find **Amagermuseet** (Amager Museum; Hovedgaden 4 & 12; www.museumamager.dk; mid-Apr–Sept Wed–Sun noon–4pm). The kitchen and bedrooms are furnished in the old style with items donated by local residents representing a strong Dutch connection in the area. Christian II (1513–23) invited a colony of Netherlands farmers to improve soil cultivation in the region, and to provide the royal table with 'as many roots and onions as are needed'. He gave the Dutch special privileges to live in Store Magleby, which for centuries was referred to as Hollænderbyen (Dutchmen's Town). They had their own judicial system and church, and developed a bizarre local costume.

The lovely 18th-century village of **Dragør** 33, 16km (10 miles) from the city, is remarkably well preserved. A walk among the half-timbered cottages with their postage-stamp-size gardens provides a vivid impression of what life was like two or more centuries ago. Beside the boat-filled harbour, a 1682 fisherman's cottage, the oldest house in the town, has been converted into **Dragør Museum** (Havnepladsen, Strandlinien 2 & 4; www.museumamager.dk; closed for renovation until summer 2020). It is devoted to local seafaring history.

Located just north of the airport, near the Kastrup metro station, the **Blue Planet National Aquarium Denmark** ③④ (http://denblaaplanet.dk; Tue–Sun 10am–6pm, Mon 10am–9pm) will delight children and adults alike with its stunning spiralling architecture and, inside, sharks, moray eels and rays all swimming in impressive glass tanks. In the Amazon section you'll be able to walk through a hot and humid rainforest populated by birds, butterflies, piranhas and anacondas.

OPEN-AIR FOLK MUSEUM AND LYNGBY LAKE

At Kongevejen 100, Kongens Lyngby, 16km (10 miles) north of the city, is **Frilandsmuseet** (www.natmus.dk; Tue–Sun 10am–4pm, July–mid-Aug until 5pm), the intriguing Open-Air Folk Museum. The museum is accessible by car along the A3 and

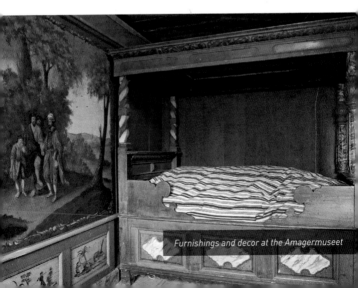

Furnishings and decor at the Amagermuseet

A5 main roads, by bus number 184 from Nørreport terminus in town, or by S-train to Sorgenfri station (leaving every 20 minutes from Copenhagen Central Station).

Over 50 farmhouses, cottages, workshops and a Dutch-type windmill are scattered about the 35-hectare (90-acre) site – all furnished in the original style, even down to combs and portraits. Broadly, the buildings are split into geographical groups laid out along country lanes, together with bridges and village pumps, and all are authentically landscaped. Each building has been transplanted, tile by tile, timber by timber, from its original location. You'll find a Zealand group, a Jutland and a Faroes group, etc. Homes of all classes are represented, from peasant to landowner, as well as artisan and farmer.

The smell of old timber and tar pervades the rooms. Geese and sheep are driven along the lanes. Displays of folk dancing, sheep shearing, threshing and weaving are given during the summer. There are horse-and-carriage rides and picnic spots in tree-lined meadows.

Allow yourself time during good weather to walk a kilometre towards **Lyngby** ㉟, where you can take a rural boat ride scarcely equalled in any capital city. On your left is the white-walled baroque castle, Sorgenfri Slot (closed to the public, although part of the gardens is accessible), built in the 18th-century by Lauridz de Thurah, who also designed the spire of Vor Frelsers Kirke (see page 62).

Proceed over Mølleåen (the Mill Stream). Follow the signs to the right for **Lyngby Sø - Bådfarten** (Lyngby Lake Boat Trip; Sorgenfrivej 23; www.baadfarten.dk) to find two venerable canopied boats at the quayside. These have plied the four lakes since the 1890s. A 45-minute cruise, either Lyngby–Frederiksdal or Lyngby–Bagsværdvej, gives you the chance to savour the tree-covered backwaters and reedy lakes. The

Houses from the past at the Open-Air Folk Museum

boats operate Tuesday to Sunday mid-June to August, weekends only May, early June and September.

As you float by, you'll pass the 1803 mansion of Marienborg amid the trees, the official summer residence of Danish prime ministers. Further on is Frederiksdal, with its castle on a hill above. This former royal house has been lived in by the same family since 1740. An alternative trip will take you to Sophienholm Mansion (1805), now a community cultural arts centre. Outdoor café tables give an idyllic view over the waters of Bagsværd Sø.

Back on Lyngby quay, the 184 bus can take you directly back into town, or it's a short walk to Lyngby S-train station.

ARKEN

Søren Robert Lund was just 25 years old and a student when he won a competition to design **Arken** 36 (www.arken.dk; Tue and Thu–Sun 10am–5pm, Wed until 9pm), to house a museum of modern art on the waterfront at Køge Bugt, 20km (12 miles) south of Copenhagen. The building gives the impression of a ship nestling in the dunes. New galleries now allow Arken to present some of its permanent collection, which emphasises art after 1990; Damien Hirst is well represented, as he donated eight pieces to the gallery in 2011. An eclectic mix of exhibitions is also staged here throughout the year. To reach Arken, take the S-train to Ishøj (lines A or E) then walk or take bus number 128 to the museum. If you want to make a full day of it, bring your swimsuit – **Ishøj Strand**, one of the metropolitan area's best sandy beaches, is close by.

LOUISIANA MUSEUM OF MODERN ART

If you have time for only one modern-art museum, make it **Louisiana** ㊲ (Gammel Strandvej 13, Humlebæk; www.louisiana.dk; Tue–Fri 11am–10pm, Sat–Sun 11am–6pm), a 30-minute train ride from Copenhagen. The museum is a work of art in itself: the main mid-19th-century mansion is extended by whitewashed galleries built into a hilly sculpture garden, with numerous glass walls blurring the boundaries between art and nature. The extensive collection includes works by Picasso, Warhol and Rauschenberg, COBRA artists such as Asger Jorn and, more recently, Per Kirkeby. A glazed corridor leads past a group of Giacometti figures to the excellent Museum Café. Its terrace – with stunning sea views – features metal mobiles by Alexander Calder. In the gardens, you can picnic on the lawns while marvelling at Henry Moore's colossal bronze women silhouetted against the waters of the Øresund. There is an excellent range of daily children's activities, too. From Copenhagen's Central Station, take the regional train (Regionaltog) to Humlebæk, in northern Zealand, from where it's a well-signposted 1km (0.6-mile) walk from the station.

HELSINGØR

Further north along the coast, at the narrowest stretch of the Øresund, is Helsingør. On leaving the railway station, the town's most famous landmark comes into view – the Unesco World Heritage site of **Kronborg Slot** ③⑧ (Kronborg Castle; www.kronborg.dk; Apr–May and Oct daily 11am–4pm, June–Sept daily 10am–5.30pm, Nov–Mar Tue–Sun 11am–4pm). To reach

Grundtvigs Kirke, an early 20th-century masterpiece

it on foot from the station takes about 20 minutes.

Many people will be familiar with Kronborg as 'Hamlet's castle of Elsinore'. No one knows if Shakespeare visited Kronborg personally, but some of his colleagues performed at the newly built castle, and so may have inspired him to set his tragedy here. Every summer the castle hosts performances of *Hamlet* in the courtyard.

The castle was built between 1574 and 1585 at the command of Frederik II for the purpose of extracting tolls from ships entering the narrow strait, and thus the Baltic (not a new idea – an earlier fortress on the site had also been a good money-spinner for the Danish treasury). Frederik, however, had more than just a stronghold in mind. He built a splendid Renaissance castle that could be lived in, peppered with ramparts, bastions, large windows and decorated towers. He sent for the Flemish architect Antonius van Opbergen to design the

Sculpture at Louisiana

four-wing structure, then engaged various Danish and Dutch artists to paint, weave and indulge in decorative sculpture on a scale never before seen in Scandinavia.

The moated brick castle today stands as Frederik's proudest memorial, now sparsely furnished but immensely impressive. It has a feeling of solid strength and royal presence throughout, permeating the elaborate little chapel, the long galleries and stone stairways, and most of all the massive oak-beamed Great Hall – the largest of its kind in northern Europe. Decked out now with 12 paintings of the Øresund by Isaac Isaacsz, its walls were once hung with 40 tapestries by the Dutchman Hans Knieper, depicting the 113 Danish kings said to have reigned before Frederik II. Fourteen of the tapestries survive, and seven can be seen in a small room beneath the hall. Underneath the castle are extensive cellars and dungeons: you can take a tour of the cramped and creepy casemates, where the castle's besieged soldiers would have crouched in the darkness. This is also where you'll find Kronborg's most renowned exhibit, the statue of the nation's own mythical hero, Holger the Dane.

Helsingør has more to offer than the castle alone: there are medieval streets of colour-washed houses, the 15th-century **Skt Mariæ Kirke** and a **Carmelite Kloster** (Convent) to see, and the shiny new **M/S Maritime Museum of Denmark** (www.mfs. dk; July–Aug 11am–6pm, Sept–June Tue–Sun 11am–5pm) with interactive exhibitions honouring Denmark's seafaring prowesses past and present. A clever architectural trick, the uneven floors and irregular angles are evocative of sailing on a vessel.

A short ferry trip across the strait to colourful Helsingborg, in Sweden, is always of interest. The Helsingør tourist office (Havnepladsen 3; www.visitnorthsealand.com), near the railway station, can supply tickets, maps and information. If you visit Helsingør on Saturday, you will come face-to-face with a social phenomenon: Swedes by the thousands making the crossing to enjoy cut-price alcohol shopping in Denmark (their own laws being strict and the prices much steeper). As a consequence, stores selling spirits, wine and beer are prevalent, and

it is a strange sight to see Swedes pushing around their little two-wheeled trolleys full of booze.

Visits to Helsingør and to the Louisiana Museum of Modern Art may be readily combined. From Helsingør, board the train for Copenhagen, alighting at Humlebæk. Alternatively, at the bus terminal next to the railway station in Helsingør board a number 388 bus for the pleasant 20-minute journey along the coast to the museum. To return to Copenhagen from Louisiana

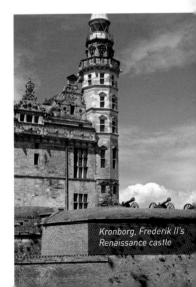

Kronborg, Frederik II's Renaissance castle

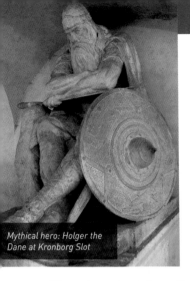

Mythical hero: Holger the Dane at Kronborg Slot

turn left onto the main road to walk back to Humlebæk railway station.

HILLERØD

Hillerød is the site of one of the greatest Renaissance castles in northern Europe, **Frederiksborg Slot** ㊴ (Frederiksborg Castle; www.dnm.dk; National History Museum daily Apr–Oct 10am–5pm, Nov–Mar 11am–3pm; gardens open daily 10am, closing at different hours depending on the season), sometimes called the Nordic Versailles. This dazzling brick and sandstone castle is dramatically situated across three islands on a lake, and the best way to reach it is by way of a small boat that departs from the city centre. Although the oldest parts of the castle date from around 1560 and were built by Frederik II, most of the castle dates from between 1600 and 1620 – the work of that visionary Builder King, Christian IV. The style is Dutch Renaissance, and the result is spectacular. Danish monarchs resided here for about a century, and the absolute monarchs were crowned in the palace chapel from 1671.

In 1859 much of the interior was destroyed by fire, but between 1860 and 1884 it was rebuilt with financial support from the brewer J.C. Jacobsen and later the Carlsberg Foundation. Since 1878 the castle has been the home of the **Danmarks Nationalhistoriske Museum** (National History Museum). This occupies more than

60 rooms and contains a complete record of the Danish monarchy, beginning with Christian I, who established the Oldenburg line (1448–1863), through all the monarchs of the following Glücksburg line to the present queen, Margrethe II. The exhibits are mostly in the form of portraits and paintings, with some pieces of period of furniture. But the rooms of the castle itself are perhaps of more interest to visitors. Riddersalen (the Knights' Hall) and the chapel are Frederiksborg's ultimate triumph. The 55m (185ft) Knights' Hall is awesome in its dimensions, with richly decorated tapestried walls, marble floor and carved wooden ceiling, all reconstructed from old drawings after the 1859 fire.

Below the Knights' Hall, Slotskirken (the chapel) escaped the fire, leaving its stunning gilt pillars and high vaulted nave virtually untouched. Almost every inch here is richly carved and ornamented. The chapel has inset black marble panels with quotations from the scriptures, marquetry panels in ebony and rare woods, and both its altar and pulpit in ebony with biblical scenes in silver relief. The organ is one of Europe's most notable, an almost unchanged original from 1610 by the Flemish master Esaias Compenius.

Around the gallery of this chapel hang the coats of arms belonging to knights of both the orders of the Elephant and the Grand Cross of Danneborg. Some modern recipients are also represented, such as Sir Winston Churchill and General Eisenhower.

Hillerød is just 9km (5 miles) from Helsingør and

Holger the Dane

Legend has it that this 9th-century Viking warrior never actually died, but just went to sleep, and will wake to defend Denmark if the country is threatened. During World War II, a section of the Resistance adopted the name of Holger Danske.

Frederiksborg Slot, home to Danish monarchs for 200 years

it is possible to visit both places in the same day (although it would make for a hurried day trip). The two towns are 30 minutes apart using the half-hourly local train (Lokalbane) service. You can travel to Hillerød from Copenhagen by S-train (on the E-line: 40-minute journey, trains every 10 minutes). Bus numbers 301, 302 and 324 go from the station to the castle.

ROSKILDE

According to legend, the Viking king Roar founded the town of **Roskilde** ⑩ around AD 600. Situated 30km (19 miles) to the west of Copenhagen, this neat little town has plenty to offer those who undertake the 25-minute train journey from the capital.

Once you arrive, head straight for the centre, towards the three green spires which dominate the flat landscape. This is Roskilde's splendid **Domkirke** (Cathedral; www.roskilde domkirke.dk; May and Sept Mon–Sat 10am–5pm, Sun 1–4pm,

June–Aug Mon–Sat 10am–6pm, Sun 1–4pm, Oct–Apr Mon–Sat 10am–4pm, Sun 1–4pm; opening times can change at short notice, so check website), a Unesco World Heritage site.

One of the most remarkable buildings in Denmark, it began life as a wooden church built by King Harald Bluetooth around AD 1000, when he first converted to Christianity. In the 1170s, Bishop Absalon, founder of Copenhagen, built a brick-and-stone cathedral here for his new bishopric, and during the course of the next 300 years this grew into the Romanesque-Gothic amalgam of today.

Christian IV added the distinctive spires in 1635. He also erected his own burial chapel and a gilded royal pew in the north wall of the church, heavily latticed and shielded from public view so that (it is said) he could smoke his pipe in peace during Sunday services. Nearly all the Danish kings and queens since Margrete I (who died in 1412) are buried in sarcophagi and chapels all different from one another in a jumbled symphony of style.

On the south side, the chapel of King Frederik V is a simple design in white paint and Norwegian marble, with 12 tombs grouped around it. In contrast, the Christian IV chapel on the north side is marked by elaborately wrought ironwork from 1618 and interior decoration mainly from the 19th century featuring frescoes, paintings depicting scenes from his reign, and bronze statues. In 2010, the medieval St Birgitte's Chapel received a very modern glass sarcophagus,

Karen Blixen

Rungstedlund, midway along the coast between the city and Helsingør, was home to *Out of Africa* author Karen Blixen. The house is now a museum devoted to her eventful life (https://blixen.dk).

designed by Bjørn Nørgaard, which will eventually hold the present queen Margrethe.

A light note is introduced by the clock high on the southwest wall of the nave: as each hour arrives, St George and his horse rear up, beneath them a dragon utters a shrill cry, a woman figure strikes her little bell four times with a hammer and a man rings his big bell once. The chapel on the outside of the cathedral beside the northwestern tower was inaugurated in 1985 and dedicated to the memory of Frederik IX, the King of Denmark from 1947–72, who is buried here.

To the front of the church is Stændertorvet, the traditional square of this old market town, lined with outdoor café tables in good weather, and fruit and vegetable stalls every Wednesday and Saturday morning. On Saturday there is also a popular flea market.

To the rear is parkland, where you can walk downhill through the meadow, towards the fjord and the **Vikingeskibsmuseet**

⊙ ACROSS THE ØRESUND TO MALMÖ

The opening in 2000 of the 8km (5-mile) long Øresund Bridge linking Denmark and Sweden has brought economic benefits to the communities on either side of the water and made the possibility of an excursion to Malmö all the more appealing. Founded in the mid-13th century, Malmö is Sweden's third-largest city. It has an attractive old town surrounding Stortorget, the main square. The Tourist Information Office (tel: 46 40 34 12 00; www.malmotown.com) at Malmö Central Station can supply maps and suggestions for walking routes. Trains leave Copenhagen Central Station every 20 minutes during the daytime, and hourly between 11pm and 6am. The journey takes 35 minutes.

(Viking Ship Museum; www.vikingeskibsmuseet.dk; daily 10am–4pm, May–mid-Oct and hols 10am–5pm). When 11th-century Danes wanted to block off the sea route to Roskilde from the marauding Norwegians, they sank five Viking ships across a narrow neck of the shallow fjord here. These ships, salvaged in 1962, now form the basis of the museum and are superbly displayed. They include a

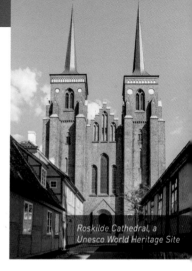

Roskilde Cathedral, a Unesco World Heritage Site

sturdy ocean-going trader and an awe-inspiring longship, the dreaded man o' war, used for long-range raiding.

The museum building stands on the edge of the water with one side made completely of glass, bringing the fjord almost into its main room. The outline of each ship was first reconstructed in metal strips, then the thousands of pieces of wood were treated and placed in position. The museum is lavishly illustrated with photographs and charts, and free film shows (in English) recount the full story of the salvage.

In recent years the Vikingeskibsmuseet has been developed into a fascinating complex in which you can see wooden boats being built by hand using the original skills, sail on one of these vessels, and eat in the attractive restaurant. Then, to end the day in a truly Viking flavour, you can sample a draught of the favourite brew of these hardy sailors, *mjød* (mead).

On the beach at Amager Strandpark

WHAT TO DO

SHOPPING

Shopping in Copenhagen is a quality experience, and the city's pedestrian precincts and attractive squares add to the pleasure of seeking out those special purchases. A host of interesting shops in the pleasant side streets and arcades around the Strøget area specialise in everything from antiques to avant-garde furniture, while established department stores such as Illum and Magasin du Nord offer the very best in Danish design.

VAT, or sales tax (in Danish MOMS), is 25 percent on all products and services. Foreign visitors (non-EU residents) who spend over 300kr in any one store displaying 'Tax-Free Shopping' stickers will be given a form to reclaim the tax when they leave the country. Ask for details in the shop, or check out the websites www.planetpayment.com or www.global-blue.com.

SHOPPING HOURS

Shopping hours vary from business to business, but general opening times are Mon–Thur 10am–6pm, Fri 10am–7pm, Sat 10am–4pm and Sun noon–4pm. A small number of shops (often food shops) are closed on Monday or Tuesday.

Certain stores stay open longer. These include bakers, florists, *smørrebrød* shops and kiosks. In addition, late-night (until 10pm or midnight) and Sunday shopping is possible at Central Station, which is like a village with a supermarket, banks open for foreign exchange, a post office, room-reservation service and snack bars.

WHERE TO SHOP

Undoubtedly the place to begin is Strøget (pronounced stroy-et), a charming pedestrian-only combination of four streets starting at Rådhuspladsen with Frederiksberggade, which leads into Nygade Vimmelskaftet, Amagertorv, Østergade, and ends in Kongens Nytorv. Along Strøget, said to be the longest pedestrian-only street in the world, you will find everything you could possibly want, and much more. The finest ceramics, silver and crystal shops, superb home furnishings and interiors stores, the city's leading furriers, antiques shops, department stores, clothing shops and souvenir outlets exist harmoniously, side-by-side with a varied selection of restaurants and bars.

In the smaller streets branching off (and parallel to) Strøget is an eclectic array of music stores, potters and silversmiths,

Shopping for antiques at City Hall Square (Rådhuspladsen)

Rådhuspladsen antiques shops and fashion boutiques. On the opposite side of Kongens Nytorv, and convenient for those visiting Amalienborg and the Marble Church, are Bredgade and Store Kongensgade. For up-and-coming designers, try bohemian Vesterbro.

GOOD BUYS

Royal Copenhagen (www.royalcopenhagen.com) is the collective name for a

A hand-painted piece by Royal Copenhagen Porcelain

group of upmarket shops located in attractive historic buildings in the heart of Strøget at numbers 4, 6, 8 and 10 Amagertorv. These are the department store Illums Bolighus for the ultimate in modern design, home furnishings and accessories; Georg Jensen Silver; Royal Copenhagen Crystal; and the world-famous Royal Copenhagen Porcelain. The last of these, founded in 1775, uses a special underglaze technique that allows landscape pastels, and even accurate skin colours, to be reproduced. All the pieces are hand-painted after a quick first firing, then fired again for glazing at 1,400°C (2,600°F). No two pieces are alike. Fans might also want to visit the Royal Copenhagen Factory Outlet (Sondre Fasanvej 5) in the suburb of Frederiksberg, which sells cheaper end-of-lines and seconds – take the Metro to Fasanvej Station, or bus no 4A or 9A.

Amber jewellery is offered everywhere, particularly in stores along Strøget. The local 'gem' (actually a fossil resin) may be cheaper here than at home, but beware, the quality can vary tremendously.

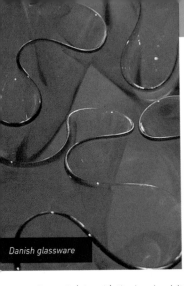
Danish glassware

Visit the House of Amber (www.houseofamber.com) at Vesterbrogade 1A or Nygade 6.

Antiques are in plentiful supply, especially the second-hand/vintage rather than the fine-art variety. The locals flock to Bredgade, off Kongens Nytorv, and Ravnsborggade, in the Nørrebro neighbourhood, which contains a dozen of antiques shops and hosts the occasional flea market.

Aquavit *(akvavit)*, the local spirit, usually flavoured with caraway seed, is cheaper than imported spirits. You'll find good prices at the airport duty-free store.

Danish furniture ranks among the world's best. Here you'll see items credited to the designer rather than to the factory. Furniture is a national pride and most good pieces will have a black circular 'Danish Furniture-Makers' sticker attached. Lamps are also lovingly designed, as are household textiles and hand-woven rugs. The best stores for sofas, chairs and tables, and the things to put on them, are: Illums Bolighus (Strøget; www.illumsbolighus.dk); CasaShop (Store Regnegade 2; www.casashop.dk); Hay House (Østergade 61; www.hay.dk); Designer Zoo (Vesterbrogade 137; https://designerzoo.dk); in Frederiksberg, CPH Square (Chr. d IX's Gade 4; www.cph square.dk); and north of Osterbrø, the designer furniture store, Paustian (Kalkbrænderiløbskaj 2; www.paustian.dk).

Knitwear comes Nordic-style, often highly patterned, warm, and, in some cases, expensive. There are knitwear shops all over the city; some sell wool and patterns for those who are tempted to set about knitting their own garments.

Stereo equipment. The very latest in sound systems, TVs and speakers can be found at the Bang & Olufsen Centre (http://stores.bang-olufsen.com), at Østergade 18.

Silver is another Danish speciality, dominated by the name Georg Jensen. Silver in Denmark is quality-controlled and should always be hallmarked. The Jensen showrooms at Amagertorv 4 offer creations that range from key rings to highly precious jewellery.

Souvenirs are myriad. Little Mermaid figures, Copenhagen dolls in frilly skirts and black lace caps, blue ceramic figurines and animals, and countless trolls and Vikings abound, as well as hand-painted spoons, racks and pepper mills. A particularly attractive Danish keepsake is an Amager shelf – a group of three or four small hand-painted shelves in a triangular frame that hangs on the wall. Beware, however, of cheap versions.

Toys are simple and attractive, especially those in solid wood. You'll also see hundreds of the Danish wooden soldiers in all sizes. Of course, when it comes to toys that are fun and educational, the Danish invention Lego is the daddy of them all – their flagship store is on Strøget (Vimmelskaftet 37; www.lego.com).

Clocks and watches. Gullacksen Ure, Frederiksberggade 8 on Strøget, may not be the largest clock shop, but its owner is the third generation

Best shopping

Check out www.visitcopenhagen.com/copenhagen/shopping for an insider's guide to some of Copenhagen's best shopping quarters.

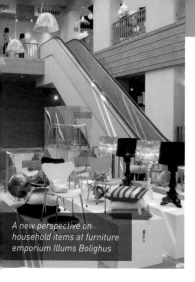

A new perspective on household items at furniture emporium Illums Bolighus

of an old watchmaking family. Besides a wide selection of Danish and international brand-name watches, clocks, barometers and hygrometers, look for the museum pieces on the walls. Of particular interest are the practical Jacob Jensen temperature stations.

ENTERTAINMENT

When in Copenhagen, relax as the Danes do. Rent a bike for a different view of life, walk in the beech woods and parks, have a night on the town at a concert or jazz club – or simply pause for a snack on one of the many public benches.

NIGHTLIFE

Classical music, opera, ballet. Scores of concerts are held throughout the year at the Royal Theatre, Tivoli, the Royal Conservatory of Music, Radio House, in churches and museums. Opera and ballet are performed at the splendid Opera House – a small number of tickets are held back for sale on the day. The Royal Danish Ballet is internationally acclaimed, and rightly so – it is one of Europe's oldest, with a repertory going back 200 years. Nowadays, the company experiments in modern dance as well, but its great tradition lies in Bournonville classics, such as *La Sylphide* and *The Dancing School*. The company performs from September to June.

Clubs and bars. Copenhagen is a great place for partying. Some of Copenhagen's cosy cafés become bars at night, and many of the city's best nightspots blur the line between bar and restaurant: often when the kitchen closes, a place will slide smoothly into 'club' mode, staying open late into the night. Alcohol is expensive, so there's a tendency for people to drink at home first and start hitting the town from 11pm onwards. 'In' places come and go, but trendy Vesterbro is the most plausible area to start: for a taste of the good life, try WarPigs (Flæsketorvet 25–37; http://warpigs.dk), a place famous for its craft Mikkeller's beers and excellent BBQ dishes. Nearby Jolene (Flæsketorvet 81–85; Thu–Sat 8pm–4/4.30am) is a quirky riot. Longstanding Vega (Enghavevej 40; www.vega.dk), a huge complex containing no fewer than 12 bars, is one of the city's biggest and best mainstream clubs. There are also several especially friendly bars in the area around the university. Locally brewed beers are popular – sample them at BrewPub (Vestergade 29; www.brewpub.dk), near the Rådhus; or at the award-winning microbrewery Nørrebro Bryghus (Ryesgade 3; www.noerrebrobryghus.dk). Also in Nørrebro is the intimate, laid-back nightclub Rust (Guldbergsgade 8; www.rust.dk), with a minimalist, sci-fi atmosphere, which hosts top DJs and has great live shows.

Jazz, folk, rock. Copenhagen is one of Europe's leading jazz centres. Jazzhus Montmartre (Regnegade 19A; www.jazzhusmontmartre.dk) is

Danes entertain

If you are fortunate enough to be invited to a Danish home, don't turn down the opportunity. The Danes love to entertain and set great store by creating a cosy yet chic atmosphere for guests.

The grand interior of the
Royal Theatre, built in 1874

one of the city's premiere venues, hosting international,
national and local artists. Mojo Blues Bar (Løngangsstræde
21C; www.mojo.dk) is another great live music venue that
is usually packed to the brim. There's an annual 10-day
Jazz Festival, which is held at the beginning of July, plus
a two-week-long Vinterjazz (http://jazz.dk) festival in
February. There are several venues for folk music near
the university.

One of the main venues for local and international rock and
pop concerts is Amager Bio (Øresundsvej 6; www.amagerbio.
dk). Big names also play at Tivoli Gardens (www.tivoli.dk) and
at Forum Copenhagen. Loppen in Christiania (www.loppen.
dk) attracts a more artistic clientele, who come to see great
local experimental, alternative, hardcore, world, jazz and rock
shows. On summer Sundays free rock concerts are held in
Fælled Park.

Cinemas. Close to Rådhuspladsen, Palads (Axeltorv 9; www.nfbio. dk), the Imperial (Ved Vesterport 4; www.kino.dk) and Dagmar (Jernbanegade 2; www.nfbio.dk) show mainstream blockbusters, and Grand Teatret (Mikkel Bryggers Gade 8; www.grandteatret. dk) shows arthouse films. Empire Bio (Guldbergsgade 29; www. empirebio.dk) offers luxury seats and plenty of legroom. Most films are shown in their original language with Danish subtitles.
Casino. Casino Copenhagen, Radisson Blu Scandinavia Hotel, 70 Amager Boulevard; www.casinocopenhagen.dk.

SPORTS

There are plenty of sporting activities to suit every taste within easy reach of the city. The top spectator sport is football (soccer), while popular participation sports include sailing and fishing. Ask the nearest Danish tourist office (see page 129) for an up-to-date list of what's available.

Cycling. Some hotels lend bicycles to their guests at no charge. Otherwise they're easy to hire (see page 117). You can use the extensive network of cycle paths *(cykelsti)* without any worry about cars, or indeed the weather – if it starts raining, country buses and trains will carry your bike and taxis have bicycle racks.

Fishing. Jutland is the Danish sea-fishing mecca, but you can still go for Øresund cod, mackerel, gar-pike, or flat-fish from Amager and the coast to the north of the city. A state angling licence costs 40/130/185kr per day/week/year and can be bought at campsites, fishing-tackle shops and tourist offices. You can rent licensed boats on Lyngby, Furesø and Bagsværd lakes on the northwest edge of Copenhagen.

Football. The Danish football team competes at the highest level, and the sport has an enthusiastic following. The main

Copenhagen stadium is at Telia Parken (www.teliaparken. dk), the home ground of F.C Copenhagen and the Danish national team.

Horse racing. The racetrack *(Galopbane)* at Klampenborg (www.galopbane.dk) is open mainly on Saturdays from mid-April–late October. To get there, take the regional train (Regionaltoget) RE2101 towards Helsingør, or the S-train, alighting at Klampenborg, then catch bus number 388 in the Lyngby direction.

Kayaking. Guided kayaking tours of Copenhagen harbour and Christianshavn's canals are available from KajakOle, tel: 40 50 40 06, https://kajakole.dk; also kayak polo at Amager Strandpark.

Sailing. Join enthusiasts sailing on the Øresund and inland lakes. Yachts and cru isers are available for hire. Evidence of navigational proficiency is required for sailing on the Øresund. Book in advance with help from your local Danish tourist office (see page 129).

Skating. Numerous stretches of water within the capital's boundaries freeze up in winter and outdoor rinks *(skøjtebaner)* are set up in the city centre, such as at Frederiksberg Runddel and Kongens Nytorv.

Swimming. There is good sea bathing along the Zealand coast north and south of Copenhagen, but the sea is rarely warm. Nude bathing is mainly at Tisvildeleje, away from the north coast. There are about a dozen indoor swimming pools in Copenhagen, some with sauna/massage and gym facilities, and several outdoor pools which are open from mid-May until the end of August. So successful has the clean-up of the Inner Harbour been that there is now a fantastically popular outdoor swimming pool at Islands Brygge (open June–Sept 7am–7pm), with diving towers and a green lawn full of picnickers in front.

Football is Denmark's most popular spectator sport

Another wonderful facility is Amager Strandpark (www.kk.dk/amagerstrandpark), a vast man-made beach and lagoon just 5km (3 miles) from the city centre, where Copenhageners flock to swim, run, skate, and play beach volleyball. There are Metro stations at three places along the beach: Øresund, Amager Strand and Femøren.

Watersports. Water-skiing is popular on the Furesø, and it is possible to windsurf in Vedbæk harbour – consult the tourist office for details. At Amager Strandpark (see above), you can rent kayaks from Kajakhotellet (http://kajakhotellet.dk) or learn to kite-surf with KiteCPH (www.kitecph.dk).

CHILDREN'S COPENHAGEN

Amusement parks. Tivoli (see page 27) should certainly appeal to the entire family. Less well known than Tivoli – and

There are plenty of rides to enjoy at Tivoli Gardens

generally considered to be a rather downmarket version – is Bakken (tel: 39 63 35 44, Apr–Aug; www.bakken.dk), which is very popular with Danes. Situated on the outskirts of Klampenborg, just a 12-minute train ride from the city centre, it has 32 rides, 40 cafés and restaurants and the country's most famous revue show. Entry to the park is free, and an all-ride pass costs 269kr.

Museums and attractions. Ripley's Believe it or Not Museum (Rådhuspladsen 57; tel: 33 32 31 31; www.ripleys.com/copenhagen) houses a collection of 'bizarre but true' exhibits. The Experimentarium Science Centre (Tuborg Havnevej 7, Hellerup, tel: 39 27 33 33; www.experimentarium.dk) is a lively place where children are positively encouraged to tinker around with exhibits. The Frilandsmuseet (see page 69) (http://natmus.dk) always goes down well with kids. At Christiansborg children can visit the Royal Stables (see page 41) and see the coaches and the horses that pull them.

Several major museums have special sections for children. These include the Nationalmuseet (see page 44), Statens Museum for Kunst (see page 51) and Louisiana (see page 72). The Danish War Museum (Tøjhusgade 3; tel: 33 11 60 37; http://natmus.dk) features a magnificent display of shining armour, model planes, giant cannons and ship models. The Viking Ship Museum at Roskilde (see page 80) has a children's section where two Viking ships may be boarded.

Copenhagen's Zoologisk Have (see page 65), established more than 120 years ago, is a good place to spend an afternoon. It houses more than 2,500 animals and has a fine children's section, restaurant and cafeteria. Den Blå Planet (The Blue Planet; Jacob Fortlingsvej 1, 2770 Kastrup; tel: 44 22 22 44; www.denblaaplanet.dk) opened in 2013 in an amazing swirl-shaped building on Amager Island (visible as you're coming in to land at the international airport). The aquarium (see page 69), a 200m/yard walk from Kastrup Metro station, contains over 17,000 animals, including piranha, sharks, sea lions and anacondas.

Swimming. Indoors, Vandkulturhuset at the DGI sports centre (Tietgensgade 65; tel: 33 29 80 00; www.dgi-byen. dk) is a state-of the-art swimming complex with facilities for children of all ages. Outdoors, the Islands Brygge harbour swimming pool (see page 92) has two children's sections.

Tours. Canal trips are a must (see page 121). Worth considering are boat cruises, such as those from Lyngby (see page 70).

Open-air swimming at Islands Brygge

CALENDAR OF EVENTS

Most of Copenhagen's annual festivals involve music. For an up-to-the-minute guide to what's on, visit the Copenhagen Visitor Centre (see page 129) or check out www.visitcopenhagen.com/search/whatson.

February Vinterjazz: three weeks of winter jazz. Frost Festival: a month of pop/electronic gigs in unusual venues around the city.

Shrovetide Beating the Barrel, parades and carnival festivities, centred around Rådhuspladsen and the Nationalmuseet. Also at Dragør on Amager island.

April Queen's birthday (16 April): crowds gather outside Amalienborg Slot at noon for the Queen's balcony appearance. CPH PIX: 10-day international film festival.

May Marches and brass bands converge on Fælled Park on May Day. Copenhagen Marathon held in May. Distortion: 100,000 ravers join a city-wide party (late May/early June).

Whitsuntide Copenhagen Carnival: colourful Latin-style processions and hundreds of bands attract large numbers of spectators.

June St Hans Eve (23 June): bonfires burn to celebrate the longest day. Roskilde Festival (late June/early July): Denmark's biggest rock festival.

July Copenhagen Jazz Festival: bands play every jazz style from bebop onwards, on stage, in pubs and on the streets.

August Copenhagen Historic Grand Prix: vintage cars take to the streets. Ballet Festival: performances by the Royal Danish Ballet. Copenhagen Pride: five-day LGBTQ event culminating in a colourful parade. Kulturhavn: harbour-based festival, with music, dancing and family fun.

September Golden Days Festival: celebrates a different era of Copenhagen's history each year with all manner of cultural events. Blues Festival: concerts at venues across the city.

October Night of Culture: museums, galleries, churches, libraries and theatres open their doors after dark and invite the public inside. Mix Copenhagen: gay and lesbian film festival.

November–December Tivoli is transformed into a winter wonderland with glittering illuminations, ice-skating and a Christmas market.

EATING OUT

Food is of a high standard in Denmark, and is a national obsession. Danes at home will happily spend two hours over their *frokost* (lunch) or up to four hours if entertaining special guests, while a celebratory *middag* (dinner) can last from 6pm to very, very late. This leisurely style of dining carries over into the cosy, welcoming café culture: sit as long as you like over a beer or coffee, and take time out to meet the Danes.

RESTAURANTS AND BARS

There are more than 2,000 restaurants, cafés, bars and snack bars in Copenhagen. Restaurants often serve a special dish of the day *(dagens ret)* and what is known as the *dan-menu* – a two-course Danish lunch or dinner for a fixed price – in addition to *à la carte* items. Keep an eye open for a *daglig kort* (daily menu), which usually features less-expensive dishes than those listed on the more formal menu *(spisekort)*. You'll also find little lunch-only, cosy cellar restaurants. These offer good value with an old-world charm, and are frequented by Danes themselves. Copenhagen has

Sleek Danish dining

more than its fair share of fine restaurants, 17 of which have been awarded Michelin stars (Noma, named world's best four times by *Restaurant* magazine, boasts two). For a drink, drop into one of the numerous cafés, pubs or bars dotted throughout the city.

Most restaurants stop serving at 9 or 10pm, and many close on Sunday/Monday. A charge is often made for using foreign credit cards. VAT and service charges are included in the bill. Danes are not tip-minded, although after a meal you may want to round up your bill. At very good restaurants, after excellent service, show your appreciation with up to a 5 percent tip.

BREAKFAST

Breakfast *(morgenmad)* in a Danish hotel is a far cry from the Spartan 'continental breakfast' of a roll and a cup of coffee. Bread rolls, cold cuts, cheeses, jam, pastries and probably eggs are all accompanied by milk and fruit juice followed by tea or coffee.

COLD DISHES

Cold food is Denmark's truly outstanding culinary speciality. *Smørrebrød* (open sandwiches) are thickly buttered slices of heavy Danish rye bread covered with one of a wide array of delicacies: liver pâté *(leverpostej)*, veal *(kalvekød)*, ham *(skinke)*, roast beef *(stegt oksekød)*, salmon *(laks)*, smoked eel *(røget ål)*, shrimp *(reje)*, cod roe *(torskerogn)*, pickled herring *(sild)*, a variety of salads *(salat)* or cheese *(ost)*. This main layer is garnished with various accessories that have been carefully chosen to enhance both taste and appearance.

Larger restaurants have scores of different *smørrebrød*. The usual procedure is to mark your orders on the menu itself, specifying which kind of bread you want (*knækbrød*: crisp-bread; *rugbrød*: rye; *franskbrød*: white; or *pumpernikkel*: black).

Herring – New Nordic-style

Don't confuse your *smørrebrød* with the Swedish word *smorgasbord*. The famous Scandinavian buffet-style spread is known in Denmark as *det store kolde bord* (the cold table), and usually offers a bewildering array of dishes. For a fixed price, you start at one end of the table, helping yourself to herring in various forms, seafood, salads and other delicacies, and go on to sample liver pâté, ham and other cuts of meat. Despite its name, the cold table always includes hot items, such as meatballs, pork sausages, soup and fried potatoes. Several kinds of bread and salads are also provided. Danish *akvavit* (see page 104) and beer go especially well with *koldt bord*.

FISH AND SHELLFISH

Fish (or small canapés) is the traditional first course of a full meal. It is also available as a main course, and a great variety of fish appears on the Danish menu. Herring is one of the firm favourites, and may be served pickled or fried, with a sherry, vinegar, curry or fennel dressing. Succulent red Greenland shrimps are also popular. Lobster is also offered – though it is not cheap – as is crab, cod and halibut. Plaice features frequently in the local cuisine and may be served boiled or fried with a garnish of shellfish or parsley.

One great Scandinavian delicacy is *gravad laks*, in which raw salmon is pressed with salt and a small amount of sugar, and then sprinkled generously with chopped dill. A creamy sauce of oil, mustard and sugar is traditionally served alongside as an accompaniment.

MEAT AND POULTRY

Although Danish meat dishes most frequently make use of pork and veal, beef has made a major breakthrough, as Danish farmers now breed more cattle. The kinds of steak that you are most likely to be offered are *fransk bøf* (fillet steak served with herb butter and French fries) and *engelsk bøf* (fillet steak served with fried onions and potatoes).

The top restaurants cook in classic French/international style. In small establishments, some typical Danish hot dishes appear on the menu such as *mørbradbøf*, a delectable legacy of the pork-only days – small cuts of tenderloin, lean, very tasty and served as a main course with boiled potatoes, onions and gravy.

Summer shrimps

A summer seafood speciality is *danske rejer*, small pink shrimps from local waters that are served piled high on white bread.

More ordinary fare – but delicious nevertheless – are Danish meatballs (*frikadeller*), a finely minced mixture of pork and veal, often served with potato salad and red cabbage. *Biksemad* is also cheap and

Noma is considered one of the world's top restaurants

tasty: a Danish hash of diced potatoes, meat and onions with a fried egg on top. A hearty Danish stew is *Hvids labskovs*, made from chunks of beef boiled with potatoes, peppercorns and bay leaves.

Chicken is most often served roasted with potatoes fried in butter and a cucumber salad *(agurkesalat)*. Roast duck is served with apple or prune stuffing and is usually accompanied by caramelised potatoes and a generous array of vegetables.

SALADS

The word for salad, *salat*, has two meanings. It can be a side dish of fresh lettuce, tomato, sliced egg and plentiful red peppers; or, more often, it's one of several mayonnaise mixtures, which are eaten on *smørrebrød* or as an appetiser. *Italiensk salat* consists of carrots, asparagus, peas and macaroni. *Skinkesalat* is basically chopped ham; *sildesalat*

Creamy desserts

comprises marinated or pickled herring, beetroot and apple. These are the most common of the many sandwich salads available.

CHEESE AND FRUIT

Danish Blue *(Danablue)*, a rich, sharp-flavoured cheese, has always had a strong international following, along with Havarti. Fynbo and Samsø, both relatively mild and firm cheeses, possess a sweet, almost nutty flavour. *Rygeost,* smoked cream cheese spiced with cumin seed, is wonderful.

DESSERTS

You will have gathered that Denmark is not a good place for dieting. And by the time you get to the desserts your best intentions will have been quite definitely routed. Desserts are usually laced with cream *(fløde)* or whipped cream *(flødeskum)*.

Favourites include: *æblekage* (stewed apples with vanilla, served with alternating layers of biscuit crumbs and topped with whipped cream) and *bondepige med slør* (a mixture of rye-bread crumbs, stewed apple, sugar and the ubiquitous whipped cream).

SNACKS

For a snack with a difference, try the deep-fried Camembert served with toast and strawberry jam *(ristet franskbrød med friturestegt camembert og jordbærsyltetøj)*. The university area is good for cheap goulashes, hashes and *håndmadder* (usually three slender *smørrebrød* with different toppings). Graze around the central Torvehallerne Market (daily 10am–7pm) to sample high-end specialist cuisine. Hot-dog stands *(pølsevogn)* are found everywhere, serving red Danish sausages *(pølse)*. Curiously, Danish pastry is known here as Viennese pastry *(wienerbrød)*: this light and flaky delight can be found in any *konditori* (bakery), and makes a delectable snack.

⊘ SKÅL! ...AND TAK!

Learn to say *skål* (the vowel is between 'loll' and 'hall') with your beer or *akvavit*. It's more than just Danish for 'cheers', it's a ritual if you are invited to a Danish home. Your host usually has the privilege of making the first toast, and will raise a glass, point it towards everyone in turn, looking directly at them, and say *'skål!'*. After all have taken a sip or a swallow, the host will look at each again in turn before putting down the glass.

After the meal itself, the appropriate – and essential – words to say are *'tak for mad'* (pronounced *'tak for maad'*), meaning, very simply, 'thanks for the meal'.

DRINKS

Street-side drinking

Golden Danish lager comes in several types: *lys pilsner* (light lager), which has only 2 percent alcohol; the more normal green-bottle pilsner; and the stouts and special beers (such as Carlsberg Elephant) at 6 to 7 percent or more. Pilsner is available everywhere almost 24 hours a day. In addition, more diverse beers have become available recently, with excellent microbrews and imported European beers widely sold.

Akvavit is fiery Danish schnapps made from potatoes, often with a caraway taste. The colour varies according to the herbs and spices that have been used for flavouring. It is sipped at mealtimes during the opening fish course or with the cheese, and will sometimes be washed down with a beer chaser. If you order *akvavit* with your meal, the bottle may occasionally be put on the table for you to help yourself. Don't be deluded into thinking you'll only be charged for a single measure – back at the bar they'll know exactly how much has gone.

All wines are imported from France, Germany or Italy, and they are always expensive in restaurants. Even cheap house wine *(husets vin)* may be three times the supermarket price. After your dinner, try the Danish cherry liqueur, *Cherry Heering*.

Coffee *(kaffe)* can be found everywhere – rich, strong and served with cream. The price may seem high, but the waiter will usually come around offering refills.

TO HELP YOU ORDER ...

Could we have a table? **Kan vi få et bord?**
Do you have a set menu? **Har De en fast menu?**
I'd like a/an/some ... **Jeg vil gerne have ...**

beer **en øl**	napkin **en serviet**
bread **brød**	pepper **peber**
coffee **kaffe**	potatoes **kartofler**
dessert **en dessert**	salad **en salat**
fish **fisk**	salt **salt**
glass **et glas**	soup **suppe**
ice cream **is**	sugar **sukker**
meat **kød**	tea **te**
menu **et spisekort**	vegetables **grønsager**
milk **mælk**	(iced) water **(is) vand**
mustard **sennep**	wine **vin**

...AND READ THE MENU

agurkesalat cucumber salad	**kylling** chicken
blomkål cauliflower	**kål** cabbage
citron lemon	**lever** liver
flæskesteg roast pork and crackling	**løg** onion
	medisterpølse pork sausage
grøn peber green pepper	**nyre** kidney
grønne bønner French beans	**oksekød** beef
gulerødder carrots	**pommes frites** French fries
hamburgerryg loin of pork	**porre** leek
hindbær raspberry	**rødkål** red cabbage
jordbær strawberry	**ssvinekød** pork
kartoffelmos mashed potatoes	**øtunge** sole
	æble apple
kirsebær cherry	**æg** egg
kotelet chop	**æggekage** omelette

PLACES TO EAT

The restaurant prices in this section are based on the cost of an average three-course evening meal (set menu) for one person, including tax but excluding drinks.

$$$$	over 600kr
$$$	400–600kr
$$	250–400kr
$	below 250kr

AROUND RÅDHUSPLADSEN AND VESTERBRO

A Hereford Beefstouw $$$ *by Tivoli, Vesterbrogade 3, DK-1620 Copenhagen V; tel: 33 12 74 41;* https://beefstouw.com/restaurants. Juicy steaks are cooked to order here. It's a restaurant chain with a difference – a percentage of the profits are invested in the quality art that adorns the restaurants. Open daily 11am–midnight.

Andersen Bakery Europe $ *Thorshavnsgade 26, DK-2300 Copenhagen S; tel: 33 75 07 35;* http://andersen-bakery-eu.dk. Excellent bakery with a Tivoli café attached: stop in for a light lunch or to try one of their renowned gourmet hot dogs. Open Mon–Fri 6.30am–7pm, Sat–Sun 6.30am–6pm.

Bang & Jensen $ *Istedgade 130, DK-1650 Copenhagen V; tel: 33 25 53 18;* www.bangogjensen.dk. A chilled-out café-bar with a bohemian vibe, Bang & Jensen is perfect for everything from breakfast to a late-night beer. There's a small menu of light home-made meals, including sandwiches, chilli con carne, pasta and baba ganoush. Open Mon–Tue 7.30am–midnight, Wed–Fri 7.30am–2am, Sat 10am–2am, Sun 10am–midnight.

BOB BioMio Organic Bistro $$ *Halmtorvet 19, DK-1700 Copenhagen V; tel: 33 31 20 00;* http://bobbistro.dk. In Copenhagen's on-trend Meatpacking District, BioMio serves healthy organic food with touches of the Far East to meat-eaters and veggies. Order your food directly from the chef in the open kitchen, and dine at sociable communal tables. Open daily noon–midnight.

Formel B $$$$ *Vesterbrogade 182, DK-1800 Frederiksberg C; tel: 33 25 10 66;* https://formelb.dk. This Michelin-starred restaurant offers an impeccable gastronomic experience. Classical French cooking is honed with Danish raw materials inspired by the modern European kitchen. Set menu. Open Mon–Thu 5.30pm–midnight, Fri–Sat until 1am.

Kodbyens Fiskebar $$ *Flæsketorvet 100, DK-1711 Copenhagen V; tel: 32 15 56 56;* http://fiskebaren.dk. This popular place in the Meatpacking District shows off Scandinavia's fish and seafood to great effect – think sea urchins from Norway, Limfjorden oysters, char from Lake Vättern. If you don't have a restaurant reservation, you might get a seat at the bar. Open Sun–Thu 11.30pm–midnight, Fri–Sat until 2am.

Mother $ *Høkerboderne 9-15, DK-1712 Copenhagen V; tel: 22 27 58 98;* www.mother.dk. You'll pay premium prices to dine in cool Kødbyen, but Mother is one of the best-value restaurants in the area, serving scrumptious sourdough pizzas to hungry crowds. Reservations are taken only up to 8pm, then it's a free-for-all. Open daily 11am–1am.

Nimb $$-$$$$ *Berstorffsgade 5, DK-1577 Copenhagen V; tel: 88 70 00 00;* www.nimb.dk. The wonderful Moorish Palace in Tivoli contains two smart bars, a pastry shop and three top-rated restaurants: the family-friendly brasserie, the Bar'n'Grill, and the Terrace, a French-inspired bistro.

PatéPaté $$-$$$ *Slagterboderne 1, DK-1716 Copenhagen V; tel: 39 69 55 57;* http://patepate.dk. Fashionable yet friendly, this relaxed restaurant in the hip Kødbyen district serves up delicious French, Spanish and Moroccan food at big shared tables. With its candlelit bistro feel and huge wine list, it really comes into its own at night. Open Mon–Wed 9am–midnight, Thu–Fri until 1am, Sat 11.30am–1am.

Rio Bravo $-$$ *Vester Voldgade 86, DK-1552 Copenhagen V; tel: 33 11 75 87;* www.riobravo.dk. A no-nonsense cowboy-style steakhouse, where even the seats at the bar are saddles. A popular place with Copenhagen's late-night revellers. Open Mon–Thu 11.30am–1am, Fri–Sat 11.30am–5am, Sun 5pm–1am.

Trois Cochons $$ *Værnedamsvej 10, DK-1619 Copenhagen V; tel: 33 31 70 55;* www.cofoco.dk. On the edge of Vesterbro and Frederiksberg, this place is worth the walk for the good-value food, attractive surroundings and its position on Copenhagen's self-confessed foodie street. Housed in an old butcher's shop, it serves up gourmet, hearty French bistro food amongst candles, chandeliers and glass-panelled cabinets. Open Mon–Fri 8am–3pm, 5.30pm–midnight, Sat–Sun 9am–3pm, 5.30pm–midnight.

STRØGET AND BEYOND

Restaurant L'Alsace $$ *Ny Østergade 9/Pistolstræde, DK-1101 Copenhagen K; tel: 33 14 57 43;* www.alsace.dk. Looking out onto a charming courtyard surrounded by 17th-century buildings, this restaurant has an interesting and diverse menu. Specialities include Iberian ham, oysters, caviar and other seafood. Open Mon–Sat 11.30am–midnight.

Café Sorgenfri $ *Brolæggerstræde 8, DK-1211 Copenhagen K; tel: 33 11 58 80;* www.cafesorgenfri.dk. In a central location just south of Strøget, this Danish diner serves *smørrebrød* and classic dishes below ground level and has a good reputation. Open Mon–Wed 11am–8pm, Thu–Sat 11am–9pm, Sun noon–6pm.

Husmann's Vinstue $$ *Larsbjørnsstræde 2, DK-1454 Copenhagen K; tel: 33 11 58 86;* https://husmannsvinstue.dk. This popular establishment serves up excellent traditional Danish lunch in a very nice ambiance. It's been housed in an old cellar since 1888. Open Mon–Fri 11.30am–6pm, Sat noon–5pm.

Kanal Caféen $ *Frederiksholms Kanal 18, DK-1220 Copenhagen K; tel: 33 11 57 70;* www.kanalcafeen.dk. Enjoy a *smørrebrød* in a maritime atmosphere at this excellent Danish lunch restaurant. Step down from street level into a warren of cosy rooms, and feast on herring, meatballs and smoked salmon from Bornholm. Open Mon–Fri 11.30am–5pm, Sat 11.30am–3pm.

Københavner Caféen $-$$ *Badstuestræde 10, DK-1209 Copenhagen K; tel: 33 32 80 81;* http://kobenhavnercafeen.dk. Handily situated just off Strøget, heading south in the direction of Gammel Strand, this place is particularly recommended for its Danish cold table and the daily Copenhagen Plate, which offers seven items for a very reasonable set price. Open daily 11am–11pm.

Kong Hans Kælder $$$$ *Vingaardsstræde 6, DK-1070 Copenhagen K; tel: 33 11 68 68;* www.konghans.dk. This lovely cellar restaurant, with its swooping Gothic arches and Michelin star, is one of Denmark's finest. It serves cuisine based on classical French dishes, freshened with new ingredients. There's a very fine wine list, and it has its own salmon smokehouse. Open Wed–Sat 6pm–midnight.

Krogs Fiskerestaurant $$-$$$ *Gammel Strand 38, DK-1202 Copenhagen K; tel: 33 15 89 15;* www.krogs.dk. In an 18th-century building with early-20th-century decor, this classic restaurant is justly renowned for its excellent fish dishes. Reservations are recommended. Open Mon–Sat 11.30am–3pm, 5am–10pm.

Madklubben $ *Store Kongensgade 66, DK-1264 Copenhagen K; tel: 33 32 32 34;* http://madklubben.dk. A riposte to the highfalutin side of the Copenhagen dining scene, Madklubben is an unpretentious place that serves fabulous food, but keeps costs low by offering a short-and-simple menu with surcharges for more expensive dishes. Near the Marble Church. Open Mon–Sat 5.30pm–midnight.

RizRaz $ *Kompagnistræde 20, DK-1208 Copenhagen K (also at Kanikkestræde 19); tel: 33 15 05 75;* www.rizraz.dk. RizRaz does a splendid Mediterranean vegetarian buffet (spinach lasagne, falafel, tabouleh etc) for 99kr at lunch, 129kr in the evening; meat-eaters can sink their canines into a burger. Heaps of tasty food for budget travellers. Open daily 11.30am–midnight.

Slotskælderen hos Gitte Kik $–$$ *Fortunstræde 4, DK-1065 Copenhagen K; tel: 33 11 15 37; www.slotskaelderen.dk.* Come to this delightful traditional lunch restaurant to feast on *smørrebrød*, served in a cosy basement. Open Tue–Sat 10am–5pm.

Tight $$ *Hyskenstræde 10, DK-1207 Copenhagen K; tel: 33 11 09 00; www.tight-cph.dk.* This classy and comfortable café-restaurant presents a small but carefully chosen selection of dishes from around the world – and every one is a winner, from the truffley mushroom soup to the sticky-toffee pudding. Open Mon–Thu 11.30am–4pm, 5–10.30pm, Fri–Sat 11.30am–4pm, 5–11pm, Sun 5–10.30pm.

UNIVERSITY QUARTER AND PARKS

42 Raw $ *Pilestræde 32, DK-1112 København K, tel: 32 12 32 10; www.42raw.com.* An informal minimalistic vegan eatery where all the dishes, including veggie burgers and salads, are heated to a maximum of 42 degrees thus keeping all vitamins and enzymes. Naturally, food is free from additives, sugar, gluten and lactose. Open Mon–Fri 8am–8pm, Sat–Sun 9am–6pm.

Café & Ølhalle 1892 $–$$ *Rømersgade 22, DK-2200 Copenhagen N; tel: 33 33 00 18; www.arbejdermuseet.dk.* This 'Café and Beer Hall' is part of Arbejdermuseet (the Workers' Museum) and offers traditional Danish grub served in an authentic 19th-century atmosphere. It also serves unique beers and aquavit, created especially for the museum by the Braunstein microbrewery. Open Mon–Sat 11am–5pm.

Det Lille Apotek $$ *Store Kannikestræde 15, DK-1169 Copenhagen K; tel: 33 12 56 06; www.detlilleapotek.dk.* Just a short walk from the Round Tower, 'The Little Pharmacy' is Copenhagen's oldest restaurant – Hans Christian Andersen is said to have dined here. It serves delicious Danish food – try the deluxe lunch-plate selection, or the juicy roast pork with crackling. Open daily 11.30am–midnight.

Geranium $$$$ *Per Henrik Lings Allé 4, DK-2100 Copenhagen Ø; tel: 69 96 00 20; www.geranium.dk.* This three Michelin-starred restaurant has a strange location, on the 8th floor of the national football stadium, Parken. Very much in the Noma vein, the food is organic, seasonal and biodynamic. Open Wed–Sat noon–4pm, 6.30pm–midnight.

Restaurant Godt $$$$ *Gothersgade 38, DK-1123 Copenhagen K; tel: 33 15 21 22;* www.restaurant-godt.dk. 'Godt' means good, which is an understatement for this small, family-run 20-seat restaurant. The cuisine is European with one daily four-course menu and a mainly French, though expanding, wine list. Open Tue–Sat 6pm–midnight.

Orangeriet $$–$$$ *Kronprinsesse 13, DK-1306 Copenhagen K; tel: 33 11 13 07;* www.restaurant-orangeriet.dk. The setting makes this restaurant – its terrace and bank of windows look out over the beautiful Kongens Have gardens. It's pricey, but on a summer's day, it's a winner for a traditional *smørrebrød* lunch. Open Mon–Sat 11.30am–3pm, 6–10pm, Sun noon–4pm.

Peder Oxe $$ *Gråbrødretorv 11, DK-1154 Copenhagen K; tel: 33 11 00 77;* www.pederoxe.dk. Danish and French cuisine is served at Peder Oxe, one of a number of fine restaurants on this attractive square. Outdoor seating, great salad bar, good wine list. Open Sun–Thu 11am–10.30pm, Fri–Sat 11am–11pm.

Restaurationen $$$$ *Møntergade 19, DK-1116 Copenhagen K; tel: 33 14 94 95;* http://restaurationen.dk. A charismatic restaurant close to the Round Tower, very much reflecting the personalities of the owners, Bo and Lisbeth Jacobsen. One fixed-price menu, featuring seasonal produce, which is changed weekly. Open Tue–Sat 6pm–midnight; closed July–Aug.

NYHAVN AND BEYOND

Els $$ *Store Strandstræde 3, DK-1255 Copenhagen K; tel: 33 14 13 41;* www.restaurant-els.dk. The elegant 19th-century decor of this delightful restaurant close to Kongens Nytorv complements the stylish cuisine. Fish is a speciality, and the menu changes with the seasons. Reservations are strongly advised. Open daily 11am–11pm.

Ida Davidsen $–$$ *Store Kongensgade 70, DK-1274 Copenhagen K; tel: 33 91 36 55;* www.idadavidsen.dk. This family-run concern in Frederiksstaden serves a staggering 250 types of *smørrebrød*, with a choice of differently flavoured *akvavit* (Danish schnapps) to accompany them. The decor is traditional. Arrive in good time to secure a table for lunch. Highly recommended. Open Mon–Fri 10.30am–5pm.

Kokkeriet $$$$ *Kronprinsessegade 64, DK-1306 Copenhagen K; tel: 33 15 27 77;* https://kokkeriet.dk. This Michelin-starred restaurant offers Danish and wider Scandinavian cuisine at its very best. Set tasting menus paired with excellent wines are excellent. Advance bookings strongly recommended. Open Mon–Sat 6pm–1am.

Lumskebugten $$$ *Esplanaden 21, DK-1263 Copenhagen K; tel: 33 15 60 29;* www.lumskebugten.dk. A small and exclusive restaurant by Churchill Park near the Little Mermaid statue, with fine food and fine wine. Vegetarians can delight in their own three-course menu – a joy in such a meat-and-fish-oriented city. Reservations are essential. Open Mon–Tue 11.30am–3pm, Wed–Sat 11.30am–3pm, 6–9.30pm.

Nyhavns Færgekro $$ *Nyhavns Færgekro, Nyhavn 5, DK-1051 Copenhagen K; tel: 33 15 15 88;* www.nyhavnsfaergekro.dk. An unpretentious restaurant serving particularly good traditional food. It's renowned for its all-you-can-eat herring buffet (119kr), with the fish prepared in 10 different ways. The location alongside Nyhavn is wonderful; you can choose to sit inside or outside depending on the weather. Open Sun–Thu 9am–10pm, Fri–Sat 9am–10.30pm.

Pastis $$ *Gothersgade 52, DK-1264 Copenhagen K; tel: 33 93 44 11;* www. bistro-pastis.dk. Locals rate this brasserie, near Kongens Nytorv, for its cosy ambiance and concise menu of fiercely French favourites – snails, *lapin provençal*, bouillabaisse. The set menu is good value for this standard of cooking. Open Mon–Thu 11am–midnight, Fri–Sat 11am–1am, Sun 11am–11pm.

Le Sommelier $$$ *Bredgade 63-65, DK-1260 Copenhagen K; tel: 33 11 45 15;* www.cph.dk. French in name and French in style, this establishment at the Copenhagen airport has a large bar and dining area. Forty wines by the glass and 1,400 in the cellar. Open daily 5am–11pm.

Studio The Standard $$$ *Havnegade 44, DK-1058 Copenhagen, tel: 72 14 88 08;* http://thestandardcph.dk. Another Michelin-star restaurant with a beautiful location on the harbourfront. Less formal than its great rival, Studio is "a workshop of passion with an inquisitive, curious and playful cuisine". Most dishes are essentially Nordic, some with an innovative Latin American twist. The cheapest five-course lunch menu costs 700kr (you will easily pay twice as much with wine), while a nine-course lunch or dinnerwhich changes with seasons will set you back 1,300kr. Guests are invited to the open kitchen to watch their dishes being prepared. Open Wed 6.30pm–midnight, Thu–Sat noon–3pm, 6.30pm–midnight.

Zeleste $$ *Store Strandstræde 6, DK-1255 Copenhagen K; tel: 33 16 06 06;* www.zeleste.dk. This delightful little restaurant is tucked away just off Nyhavn, but you won't miss it as long as they continue to hang a great big kitsch shrimp outside. In summer eat out in the courtyard; in winter, the small traditional rooms are appealingly cosy. They specialise in seafood and hearty meat dishes, such as rack of lamb or Argentine striploin. Open Sun–Thu 11am–10.30pm, Fri–Sat 11am–11pm.

CHRISTIANSHAVN AND HOLMEN

Era Ora $$$$ *Overgaden Neden Vandet 33B, DK-1414 Copenhagen K; tel: 32 54 06 93;* www.era-ora.dk. Opened in 1983, this Michelin-starred restaurant offers innovative gourmet Italian cuisine. Lunch menus are 2, 3, 4 or 5 courses, while the evening dining experience takes you on a 'journey' of inventive and surprising courses – a short trip is 980kr, while the longest travels are 1,280kr. Open Mon–Sat lunch and dinner.

Noma $$$$ *Strandgade 93, DK-1401 Copenhagen K; tel: 32 96 32 97;* www. noma.dk. Noma has two Michelin stars, and was named the world's best restaurant in 2010, 2011, 2012 and 2014 by *Restaurant* magazine (as of 2019 it was ranked second). As you may imagine, it's tough to get a table and reservations are taken two months in advance. Those lucky enough to get in can experience the tasting menu (2,500kr) inspired by Nordic delicacies, depending on a season, of horse mussels, deep-sea crabs and langoustines, truffles and musk ox, alongside the best beef, lamb and elderberries and the purest water from Greenland. Open Tue–Fri 5pm–midnight, Sat 11.30am–7pm.

Spiseloppen $$ *Badsmandsstræde 43, Christiania, DK-1407 Copenhagen K; tel: 32 57 95 58;* http://spiseloppen.dk. This super-cosy restaurant, run as a collective, has a daily changing menu, influenced by styles and fla-vours from all over the world. It's above the Loppen club – don't be put off by the scary-looking stairs. Open Tue–Sat 5–10.30/11.30pm.

Restaurant Viva $$ *Langebrogade Kaj 570, DK-1411 Copenhagen K; tel: 27 25 05 05;* www.restaurantviva.dk. Based inside a ship moored in the harbour by Langebro, this seafood restaurant seats 70 inside and an-other 50 on the sun deck in the summer. It offers plenty of shellfish spe-cialities, stylish decor and the sensation of being on board a ship when a passing speedboat raises waves. Open Tue 11.30am–5pm, Wed–Sat 11.30am–10pm; closed mid-end July.

NØRREBRO

Kiin Kiin $$$$ *Guldbergsgade 21, DK-2200 Copenhagen N; tel: 35 35 75 55;* www.kiin.dk. 'Eat Eat' in Thai, this restaurant on trendy Sankt Hans Square in Nørrebro has earned the highest reviews in the Danish media and is the only Thai restaurant in the world with a Michelin star. The set tasting menu is made up of creative dishes exploding with flavour. Open Mon–Sat dinner.

Radio $–$$ *Julius Thomsens Gade 12, DK-1632 Copenhagen V; tel: 25 10 27 33;* http://restaurantradio.dk. Set up in 2011 by Noma founder Claus Meyer, Radio has won endless plaudits from the Danish media for its fabulous food. Prices are kept reasonable by packing in the tables, and turning over several sittings every night. On the border of Frederiks-berg and Nørrebro, near the Forum Metro station. Open Tue–Sat from 5.30pm. also lunch Fri–Sat.

A–Z TRAVEL TIPS

A SUMMARY OF PRACTICAL INFORMATION

A

ACCOMMODATION (See also Youth Hostels and see page 133 for Recommended Hotels)

Hotels belonging to the Association of the Hotel, Restaurant and Tourism Industry in Denmark (HORESTA; www.horesta.dk) are classified on a scale of one to five stars, based on facilities offered. The Copenhagen Visitor Centre (see page 129) can book accommodation for a 100kr fee.

Rooms in private homes are listed by Dansk Bed & Breakfast (www.bedandbreakfast.dk); but note that, in spite of the name, breakfast is rarely included! Visitors on longer breaks might consider an apartment: the Hay 4 You (Knabrostræde 15, ground floor; tel: 26 28 08 25; www.hay4you.com) agency offers a variety of cosy local choices.

How much is a room for one person/two people? **Hvad koster et enkeltværelse/dobbeltværelse?**
Is breakfast included? **Er der morgenmad?**

AIRPORT

Copenhagen Airport, Kastrup (CPH; www.cph.dk), around 10km (6 miles) southeast of the city centre, is the main northern European hub.

There are trains every 10 minutes to Hovedbanegård, Copenhagen's Central Station; and the Metro runs roughly every 4–6 minutes (15–20 minutes at night) into the city centre. Both leave from Terminal 3 (where all passengers go for baggage reclaim and customs), take about 14 minutes and cost 38kr. Buses (no. 5A) run less frequently and take about 30–35 minutes.

Taxis take 20–30 minutes; expect to pay 250–300kr, depending on the time of day.

B

BICYCLE RENTAL

Copenhagen's Bycyklen city bike scheme (http://bycyklen.dk) has a fleet of white bikes kitted out with a GPS which can be hired on a pay-as-you-go or monthly basis (first half hour is free). Many hotels offer guests free bicycles. You can also rent a decent bike from a bike shop, such as Københavnhavns Cykelbørs (tel: 33 14 07 17; www.cykelboersen.dk) or Pedal Atleten (tel: 70 70 75 13; http://pedalatleten.dk). This costs about 90kr per day for a three-speeder (plus a refundable deposit). Bikes can be put on S-tog trains except during rush hours. Look for carriages with a cycle symbol.

BUDGETING FOR YOUR TRIP

Money-saving tips. Many museums (including the National Museum) are free, or have one day a week where admission is free. A Copenhagen Card (see page 130) can be good value, depending on which sights you see and how much public transport you use. To save money on a bus tour, hop on bus 1A, which runs across much of the city centre for the price of a normal bus ticket. Many restaurants offer a good-value *dagens ret* (daily special).

C

CAR HIRE (see also Driving)

Having a car in Copenhagen is a hindrance rather than a help. The public-transport system is superb, and car rental, fuel and parking costs are quite high.

If you decide to hire a car once you are in Copenhagen, you could contact Avis, tel: 70 24 77 07, www.avis.dk; Europcar, tel: 32 50 30 90, www.europcar.dk; Hertz, tel: 33 17 90 00, www.hertzdk.dk; or Budget, tel: 33 55 05 00, www.budget.dk. You will need a valid national (or international) driving licence and must be at least 19 years of age (25 for some companies). Most agencies require payment by credit card.

CLIMATE

Denmark's relatively temperate climate is due to its situation and the sea currents, but frequent switches in the wind also bring changeable weather. Spring may come late, but summer is often sunny and autumn mild. You can check the weather forecast at www.dmi.dk. Average monthly temperatures in Copenhagen are:

	J	F	M	A	M	J	J	A	S	O	N	D
°C	1	0	2	6	11	16	17	16	13	9	5	2
°F	33	32	35	42	52	60	63	61	56	48	40	36

CLOTHING

Danes have a relaxed dress code, with the smart-casual look suitable for nearly every occasion.

Summer nights are long and light but often chilly; bring a cardigan and a light raincoat in addition to ordinary summer clothes. On the beach, you can be as undressed as you like. Pack plenty of warm clothes (plus a raincoat) for winter. In all seasons, comfortable walking shoes are highly recommended for your excursions on foot around town.

CRIME AND SAFETY (See also Emergencies and Police)

Despite the 2015 terrorist attack which resulted in two fatalities, Copenhagen remains one of the safest capital cities in Europe. Pickpocketing rises during the summer months: take normal precautions, particularly in crowded areas.

D

DRIVING

If you take your car into Denmark from the UK then you will need a valid driver's licence, car registration papers, a Green Card, a red warning triangle in case of breakdown and a national identity sticker for your car. British car-owners should note that left-dipping headlights are illegal. Headlights are compulsory at all hours. Drive on the right, pass on the left.

Drinking and driving. The law is stringent: if you are discovered to have a blood-alcohol content of more than 0.05 percent while driving, you face severe penalties.

E

ELECTRICITY

The supply for electrical appliances in Denmark is 220 volt, 50 Hz AC, and requires standard two-pin, round continental plugs. Visitors should bring their own adaptors.

EMBASSIES AND CONSULATES

The embassies, with consulate sections, are generally open Mon–Fri 8am–4pm, but there is usually a 24-hour telephone service. New Zealand does not have an embassy in Denmark.

Australia: embassy: Dampfærgevej 26, 2nd floor, DK-2100 Copenhagen Ø; tel: 70 26 36 76; www.denmark.embassy.gov.au.

Canada: embassy: Kristen Bernikowsgade 1, DK-1105 Copenhagen K; tel: 33 48 32 00; www.canadainternational.gc.ca.

Republic of Ireland: embassy: Østbanegade 21, DK-2100 Copenhagen Ø; tel: 35 47 32 00; ww.dfa.ie/irish-embassy/denmark/.

South Africa: embassy: Gammel Vartov Vej 8, DK-2900 Hellerup; tel: 39 18 01 85; http://www.dirco.gov.za/copenhagen.

UK: embassy: Kastelsvej 36–40, DK-2100 Copenhagen Ø; tel: 35 44 52 00; www.gov.uk/world/organisations/british-embassy-copenhagen.

USA: embassy and consulate: Dag Hammarskjölds Allé 24, DK-2100 Copenhagen Ø; tel: 33 41 71 00; https://dk.usembassy.gov.

EMERGENCIES (See also Police and Health and Medical Care)

The all-purpose emergency number is 112 and is free from public phone boxes. Ask for police, fire or ambulance. Speak distinctly (English will be understood) and state your number and location.

To speak with a doctor during the day, ask your hotel to help. After hours (4pm–8am) and weekends, call the on-call GP on 38 69 38 69. There is also a 24-hour, 365-day helpline staffed by nurses who can advise on medical questions, and tell you which emergency clinic has the shortest waiting time – tel: 1813.

Dental emergency. Tandlægevagten, Oslo Plads 14, tel: 1813 or 70 25 00 41, is a walk-in centre for out-of-hours dental emergencies, open Mon–Fri 8–9.30pm, Sat–Sun and public holidays 10am–noon and 8–9.30pm. Cash payment only.

Can I use your phone? **Må jeg låne din telefon?**
I have lost my bag/wallet. **Jeg har mistet min taske/tegnebog.**

G

GETTING THERE

Air travel. The following airlines are among those operating regular services to Copenhagen **from the UK** (the phone numbers given are for calling from the UK): SAS (Scandinavian Airlines System; tel: 0871 226 7760; www.flysas.com), Norwegian Air (tel: 0330 828 0854; www.norwegian.com), British Airways (tel: 0844 493 0787; www.britishairways.com), easyJet (tel: 0330 365 5000; www.easyjet.com) and Ryanair (tel: 0871 246 0000; www.ryanair.com).

From the USA and Canada: SAS (Scandinavian Airlines System; tel: 1-800-221-2350 (if calling from within the USA or Canada); www.flysas.com) operates daily flights to Copenhagen from Chicago, Newark, Washington and San Francisco. Air Canada (tel: 1-888 247 2262 (if calling from within the USA or Canada; www.aircanada.com) has a regular service from Toronto.

From Australia and New Zealand: Flights to Copenhagen necessitate two, sometimes three, changes, usually in the Far East and then Europe.

Rail travel. You can travel to Copenhagen by the Eurostar from St Pancras International, London, to Copenhagen (Oui Sncf; https://en.oui.sncf), via Brussels and Cologne.

GUIDES AND TOURS

The Association of Authorised Guides offers individual and group tours (tel: 33 11 33 10; www.guides.dk; Mon, Wed, Fri 11am–4pm).

Canal and harbour tours. Canal Tours Copenhagen (tel: 32 96 30 00; www.stromma.dk) and Netto Boats (tel: 32 54 41 02; www.havnerundfart.dk) run 60-minute guided canal tours mid-January to mid-December, with around two to five departures per hour. Boats run from 10am to 7pm in July and Aug, shorter hours during the rest of the year. Canal Tours Copenhagen boats depart from Nyhavn and Gammel Strand; Netto tours depart from Nyhavn and Holmens Church. Strömma also runs the 'hop-on-hop-off' boat, with a free audioguide. Kayak Tours (tel: 40 50 40 06; www.kajakole.dk) depart from Gammel Strand for 1.5 to 3-hour canal voyages in kayaks equipped with intercom.

City tours. City Sightseeing (tel: 32 96 30 00; www.stromma.dk) 'hop-on-hop-off' bus tours depart from in front of the Radisson Blu Royal Hotel at Rådhuspladsen (City Hall Square) five minutes past the hour from 9am to 2pm. The company also runs City & Harbour Tours, combined bus-and-boat tours Tickets are valid 1 to 48 hours.

Cycling and running. Several companies offer guided bike tours, including a three-hour whiz round the city with Bike-Mike (tel: 26 39 56 88; www.bikecopenhagenwithmike.dk). For energetic types there are also jogging tours (try https://gorunningtours.com or www.runningtours.dk).

Trips to Sweden. An 'Øresund Rundt' ('Around the Sound') ticket (249kr) gives you 48 hours to make a Malmö-Helsingborg-Helsingør-Copenhagen round trip, using the Øresund Bridge in one direction and the ferry in the other: purchase it from Copenhagen Visitor Centre.

H

HEALTH AND MEDICAL CARE

Make sure your health insurance covers any illness or accident while travelling.

In Denmark, treatment and even hospitalisation is free for any tourist taken suddenly ill or involved in an accident. For minor treatments, doctors, dentists and pharmacists will charge on the spot. For EU members, this money will be partly refunded at the local Danish health service office on production of receipts and a European Health Insurance Card (EHIC; www.ehic.org.uk), obtainable online.

A Danish pharmacy *(apotek)* is strictly a dispensary. Pharmacies are listed in the phone book under *Apoteker*. Opening hours are generally Mon–Fri 9am–5.30pm, Sat until 1pm. An all-night service operates at Steno Apotek, Vesterbrogade 6C, tel: 33 14 82 66, near the main train station.

I need a doctor/dentist. **Jeg har brug for en læge/ tandlæge.**

L

LANGUAGE

English is widely spoken and understood. Danish is almost impossible to pronounce simply by reading the words, as many syllables are swallowed rather than spoken. Thus the island of Amager becomes Am-air, with the 'g' disappearing, but in a distinctively Danish way difficult for the visitor to imitate. The letter 'd' becomes something like a 'th', but with the tongue placed behind the lower teeth, not the upper. The letter 'ø' is like the 'u' in English 'nurse', but spoken with the lips far forward. And the letter 'r' is again swallowed.

There are 29 letters in the Danish alphabet including 'æ' (as in egg), 'ø', and 'å' (as in port). They appear after the usual 26 (a point to note when looking up names in phone books and lists).

Days

Monday **mandag**
Tuesday **tirsdag**
Wednesday **onsdag**
Thursday **torsdag**
Friday **fredag**
Saturday **lørdag**
Sunday **søndag**

Months

August **august**
September **september**
October **oktober**
November **november**
December **december**
January **januar**
February **februar**
March **marts**
April **april**

May **maj**
June **juni**
July **juli**

Numbers

0 **nul**
1 **en**
2 **to**
3 **tre**
4 **fire**
5 **fem**
6 **seks**
7 **syv**
8 **otte**
9 **ni**
10 **ti**
11 **elleve**
12 **tolv**
13 **tretten**
14 **fjorten**
15 **femten**
16 **seksten**
17 **sytten**
18 **atten**
19 **nitten**
20 **tyve**
30 **tredive**
40 **fyrre**

50 **halvtreds**
60 **tres**
70 **halvfjerds**
80 **firs**
90 **halvfems**
100 **hundrede**
1000 **tusind**

LGBTQ TRAVELLERS

Denmark was the world's first country to recognise same-sex part-nerships and Centralhjørnet, in Copenhagen, is the world's oldest existing gay bar. The city has a thriving gay scene, with bars, clubs and hotels openly welcoming the gay community. In 2021, Copenha-gen will host WorldPride. For information, contact LGBT Denmark, Nygade 7; tel: 33 13 19 48; www.lgbt.dk.

LOST PROPERTY

The general lost-property office *(hittegodskontor)* is at the police station at Slotsherrensvej 113, Vanløse (tel: 38 74 88 22; Mon–Fri 9am–2pm). For property lost on trains, contact the S-train informa-tion office (tel: 24 68 09 60; daily 10am–1pm). For property lost on a plane, call the Copenhagen Air Service (tel: 32 47 47 25; daily 8am–8pm). For missing credit cards: American Express, tel: +44 1273 696 933; Diners Club, tel: +44 1252 513 500. To block Visa, MasterCard and other cards: PBS 24-hour hotline, tel: 44 89 27 50.

M

MEDIA

Newspapers and magazines. English-language newspapers and magazines are widely available at news-stands, shops and hotels. *The Copenhagen Post* (http://cphpost.dk), which comes out weekly, and *The Murmur* (http://murmur.dk) monthly magazine are the main sources of information on Denmark and Copenhagen in English. The former also has a good listings guide. Some Danish dailies such as *Jyllands-Posten* (http://jyllands-posten.dk) have English sections.

MONEY

Currency. The unit of Danish currency is the kroner, abbreviated to kr, or, abroad, DKK (to distinguish it from the Norwegian and Swedish kroner). It is divided into 100 øre. Coins: 50 øre; 1, 2, 5, 10 and 20 kroner. Banknotes: 50, 100, 200, 500 and 1,000 kroner.

Credit cards and traveller's cheques. Most institutions will accept payment by most international credit cards, though many smaller shops and some restaurants (including expensive ones) will not, unless you pay a surcharge (up to 4 percent of the bill). Credit cards are not accepted in many pharmacies.

Tax. Danish VAT is called MOMS and is set at 25 percent. It's always included in the bill. Foreign visitors can claim a tax refund if they spend over 300kr in a single shop displaying the Global Tax-Free Shopping sign. Ask the cashier for a tax-free form, then take it to Planet Payment (www.planetpayment.com) or Global Blue (www.globalblue.com), who have desks in the airport and the large department stores, for a 20 percent refund. Alternatively, you can post your tax-free form.

Do you accept credit cards? **Godtager I kreditkort?**
Can you change a traveller's cheque for me? **Kan jeg indløse en rejsecheck?**

O

OPENING TIMES

Banks. Open Mon–Fri 10am–6pm, Thu until 5.30pm. In the provinces, hours fluctuate from town to town.

Museums. Often closed on Monday and generally open for shorter hours during the winter. Most museums open 10am–5pm.

Shops. Hours vary from business to business, but general opening times are Mon–Thu 10am–6pm, Fri 9am–8pm, Sat 9am–5pm; supermarkets, some boutiques and corner shops are also open on Sun.

P

POLICE (See also Emergencies)

State and city police all form part of the national force and are dressed in dark-blue uniforms. Most policemen patrol in dark-blue-and-white or white cars with the word *politi* in large letters. Police are courteous and speak English.

Where's the nearest police station? **Hvor er den nærmeste politi-station?**

The all-purpose emergency number is 112. For non-emergencies, you can also phone 114 to be connected to the nearest local police station. Main Copenhagen police station: Politigården, Polititorvet 1, tel: 33 14 14 48.

POST OFFICES

In general, post offices are open 9 or 10am–5 or 6pm during the week; some post offices are also open on Sat 9am–noon.

There is a very central post office at Pilestræde 58 (by the Round Tower; Mon–Fri 8.30am–7pm, Sat 8.30am–2pm). In Østerbro district, there's a large post office at Øster Allé 1 (the ENIGMA museum; Mon–Fri 11am–6pm, Sat 10am–2pm). All post offices display a red sign with a crown, bugle and crossed arrows in yellow – and a sign saying *Kongelig Post og Telegraf.*

PUBLIC HOLIDAYS

Though Denmark's banks, offices and major shops close on public holidays, museums, cafés and tourist attractions will mostly be open. Although Christmas Eve and New Year's Eve are not official holidays, most shops, businesses and attractions close on those days too.

1 January Nytårsdag New Year's Day

5 June (half-day) Grundslovsdag Constitution Day

25/26 December Christmas

Moveable dates:

Skærtorsdag Maundy Thursday

Langfredag Good Friday

Anden påskedag Easter Monday

Store Bededag General Prayer Day (fourth Friday after Easter)

Kristi himmelfartsdag Ascension Day

Anden pinsedag Whit Monday

T

TELEPHONES

The country code for Denmark is 45. Local Danish numbers have eight digits, and there are no area codes.

To call Denmark from the UK: dial 00 + 45 + the personal telephone number.

To make international calls from Denmark: dial 00 + the country code + the area code (omitting the first 0 for UK numbers) + the personal telephone number.

Mobile telephones. Danish mobile phones operate on the 900/1800 MHz GSM network – most unlocked European phones will work. US visitors will only be able to use their mobile in Denmark if it is a tri-band phone that can switch bands.

Public telephone boxes. Generally take prepaid telephone cards, which can be purchased from kiosks, supermarkets and petrol stations. Some take credit cards and coins.

TIME ZONES

Denmark operates on Central European Time (GMT + 1). In summer, the clock is put one hour ahead (GMT + 2). The time differences are:

New York	London	**Copenhagen**	Jo'burg	Sydney
7am	noon	**1pm**	1pm	9pm

TIPPING

Tipping is not obligatory in Denmark, as most hotel and restaurant staff are paid proper salaries.

TOILETS

Facilities are usually indicated by a pictograph; alternatively they are marked WC, *Toiletter, Damer/Herrer* (Ladies/Gentlemen), or just D/H. There is no charge unless you see it clearly marked otherwise.

TOURIST INFORMATION

The Copenhagen Visitor Centre, 4a Vesterbrogade, across from Central Station and just outside Tivoli (Oct–Feb Mon–Sat 9am–4pm, Sun 9am–2pm, Mar–Apr daily 9am–4pm, May–June and Sept Mon–Sat 9am–6pm, Sun 9am–4pm, July–Aug Mon–Fri 9am–8pm, Sat–Sun 9am–6pm, tel: 70 22 24 42; www.visitcopenhagen.com), offers a comprehensive array of tourist information, and assistance with booking sightseeing tours and accommodation.

Copenhagen Card. The Copenhagen Visitor Centre is also one of the many places where you can purchase the Copenhagen Card. The card lasts for 24, 72 or 120 hours and gives free or reduced admission to more than 80 popular museums and sights in the city. It also grants free travel on buses, S-trains, Metro and the harbour bus throughout the region, as well as discounts on car hire and the Scandlines Helsingør-Helsingborg ferry service between Denmark and Sweden. The 24/48/72/120-hour cards cost 399/599/739/989kr (children 10–15 years 199/299/369/499kr), and two children under 10 years may accompany each adult free of charge.

UK: VisitDenmark, e-mail: london@visitdenmark.com; www.visitdenmark.com.

TRANSPORT

An excellent integrated public-transport system covers not only Copenhagen but also its extensive metropolitan area. The area is divided into zones, with fares charged according to how many zones you pass through. The system makes travel simple: the same tickets are used on buses, S-trains, the harbour bus and the Metro. A basic ticket permits travel within two zones for one hour and costs 24kr (12kr for children aged 0–15). You must clip your ticket when you get on the bus, or on the train platform before you get on. A 24-hour all-zone ticket costs 130kr (65kr for children) and permits 24 hours of unlimited travel. A 24, 48, 72, 96 or 120-hour City Pass Small (zones 1–4 including to/from airport) gives unlimited access to buses, trains, metro and harbour buses and costs 80–300kr (adult) and 40–150kr (under 16s). A 24, 48, 72, 96 or 120-hour City Pass Large gives unlimited access to buses, trains, metro and harbour buses in all zones (zones 1–99 including Roskilde and Elsinore) and costs 160–600kr (adult) and 80–300kr (under 16s) (https://dinoffentligetransport.dk/citypass). All tickets and travel cards can be bought at most stations, kiosks, online on www.dsb.dk or using the DOT Mobilbilletter application (download from App Store or Google Play).

Buses. Operated by Movia (tel: 36 13 14 00; www.moviatrafik.dk), buses run daily between 6am and 12.30am. There are additional night buses from Rådhuspladsen to the suburbs. Buses are yellow and you get on at the front and off at the back.

Harbour Bus. The blue-and-yellow boats (www.moviatrafik.dk) run six times an hour (6am–6pm) through the harbour, between the Royal Library on Christians Brygge and the Little Mermaid, with stops at Nyhavn and Holmen North.

Metro. Automated Metro trains (tel: 70 15 16 15; http://intl.m.dk) run on two lines – M1 and M2 – every 4–6 minutes in the daytime, and every 15–20 minutes through the night. The Copenhagen metro system is constantly expanding with the Nordhavn extension expected to be inaugurated by 2020 and the Sydhavn extension – by 2024.

S-Train. Operated by DSB S-Tog (tel: 33 14 17 01; www.dsb.dk), the red S-tog local trains connect Copenhagen with other towns on Sjælland.

Taxis. Taxis are recognisable by a *Taxi* or *Taxa* sign, and vacant cabs display the word *fri* (free). Tipping is not necessary, but round the sum up if you are impressed by the service. The basic fare is around 30–40kr, plus 8.5–10kr per km. Fares are considerably higher at night. Most drivers accept credit cards.

Trains. A comprehensive and generally punctual network, which covers the entire country, operates from Copenhagen Central Station.

How much is a ticket to...? **Hvad koster en billet to...?**
One ticket to..., please. **En billet til..., tak.**
Where does this train/bus go? **Hvor kører dette tog/denne bus hen?**

TRAVELLERS WITH DISABILITIES

The Danes are generally very thoughtful about the needs of travellers with disabilities. God Adgang (http://godadgang.dk) is an Accessibility Label Scheme that keeps a searchable database of hotels, restaurants, shops, performance venues and tourist attractions that are accessible to people with disabilities.

Trains are equipped with lifts and ramps, and have disabled toilets. All Metro stations have lifts and most buses have collapsible ramps for the middle doors and a call button.

V

VISAS AND ENTRY REQUIREMENTS

Visitors from Britain and countries outside the EU need a valid passport to enter Denmark; citizens from EU countries, excluding Britain, need only an identity card. Visitors from the UK, USA, EU, Australia and New Zealand are generally entitled to stay in Denmark for up to 90 days without a visa.

South African citizens need a visa. See the Danish Embassy in South Africa website for further information: http://sydafrika.um.dk.

W

WEBSITES AND INTERNET ACCESS

There is comprehensive tourist information at www.visitcopenhagen. com. Catch up with the Danish news in English at *The Copenhagen Post* website http://cphpost.dk, and investigate the quirks of Danish society at http://denmark.dk. Discover Copenhagen's hottest exhibitions, music, film, theatre and sports shows on www.kulturnaut.dk.

Many cafés and hotels offer WiFi. There is also free internet access in Danish libraries and the Visitors Centre.

Y

YOUTH HOSTELS

There are 22 youth hostels in the city, four of which are run by Danhostel Danmarks Vandrerhjem, Vodroffsvej 32, 1900 Frederiksberg; tel: 31 31 36 12; www.danhostel.dk. A dorm bed costs around 170–250kr.

RECOMMENDED HOTELS

Most of Copenhagen's hotels are clustered near the city's main sights – Rådhuspladsen, Tivoli Gardens, the University Quarter and the lively shopping area along Strøget.

The following hotels are listed alphabetically, area by area. The price categories are based on the cost per night of a double room with bath or shower in the high season, including service charges and tax (but not breakfast, which is usually an extra, costing 100kr to 180kr). However, rates are often based on demand and can vary hugely: even at expensive hotels, they can be as much as 50 percent lower at other times of the year. Look out for deals or ring to ask if any are available. Booking online (and also via comparison sites) can also be cheaper.

It is always advisable to reserve ahead of your stay. The city is at its busiest in the summer months (June–August), but conferences ensure that hotels are kept busy throughout the year.

Check out the excellent overview on www.visitcopenhagen.dk, where you can also make bookings.

$$$$	over 2,000kr
$$$	1,500–2,000kr
$$	1,000–1,500kr
$	under 1,000kr

AROUND RÅDHUSPLADSEN AND VESTERBRO

66 Guldsmeden $ *Vesterbrogade 66, DK-1620 Copenhagen V; tel: 33 22 15 00;* http://guldsmedenhotels.com. A great little three-star hotel, decorated in cosy colonial style and located in the lively Vesterbro neighbourhood. Equally charming is sister-hotel *Bertrams Hotel Guldsmeden* ($$; Vesterbrogade 107; tel: 70 20 81 07), with a relaxing courtyard garden, a few blocks further down Vesterbrogade. Both provide tasty organic breakfasts with bread from a nearby gourmet bakery. 66 Guldsmeden 74 rooms; Bertrams 47 rooms.

Hotel Alexandra $$$ *H.C. Andersens Boulevard 8, DK-1553 Copenhagen V; tel: 33 74 44 44; www.hotelalexandra.dk.* This lovely old hotel, in a building originating from the 1880s, is almost next door to Rådhuspladsen. It's stylishly decorated with Danish 1950s and 60s vintage furniture, with light, airy rooms and excellent facilities. 61 rooms.

Andersen Hotel $$$–$$$ *Helgolandsgade 12, DK-1653 Copenhagen V; tel: 33 31 46 10; www.andersen-hotel.dk.* A popular, cheerful little boutique hotel. Rooms are on the cosy side: if you like your space, plump for a deluxe or junior suite. Some internet rates include a fabulous breakfast. The hotel is handy for the stylish restaurants in the old Meatpacking District (Kødbyen). 69 rooms.

Hotel Astoria $ *Banegårdspladsen 4, DK-1570 Copenhagen V; tel: 70 23 56 35; www.astoriahotel-copenhagen.com.* Dating from 1936, this budget hotel's bizarre facade is an excellent architectural example of Cubist style. It's right next to the main train station, so light sleepers may struggle in rooms on the track side. 94 rooms.

Comfort Hotel Vesterbro $–$$$ *Vesterbrogade 23–29, DK-1620 Copenhagen V; tel: 33 78 80 00; www.nordicchoicehotels.dk.* This modern hotel has a great location in trendy Vesterbro. The rooms are modern and a good size. Friendly and professional service. Just a five-minute walk from Rådhuspladsen. 400 rooms.

Copenhagen Downtown Hostel $ *Vandkunsten 5, DK-1467 Copenhagen K; tel: 70 23 21 10; http://copenhagendowntown.com.* The pick of the central hostels, this friendly, funky place has excellent facilities. The lively bar is a great place to meet fellow travellers, or you can borrow iPads and laptops from reception to contact the folk back home.

Copenhagen Marriott Hotel $$$$ *Kalvebod Brygge 5, DK-1560 Copenhagen V; tel: 88 33 99 00; www.marriott.com/cphdk.* A luxury glass and concrete block offers all that one expects from Marriott hotels, including some of the biggest rooms in Copenhagen. Waterside rooms overlook the inner harbour. 406 rooms.

Copenhagen Plaza $$$$ *Bernstorffsgade 4, DK-1577 Copenhagen V; tel: 33 14 92 62;* https://ligula.se/da/profilhotels. Commissioned by Frederik VIII in 1913, this hotel has old-fashioned style and a historic elevator with a mind of its own! Rooms are decently-sized – reserve one on a higher floor for impressive city views. The wood-panelled, leather-seated Library Bar has its own jazz pianist and professional cocktail-maker. Breakfast included. 93 rooms.

Hotel Danmark $$ *Vester Voldgade 89, DK-1552 Copenhagen V; tel: 33 11 48 06;* www.brochner-hotels.dk. Adjacent to Rådhuspladsen and close to Strøget, this hotel is housed in two buildings, with rooms tastefully furnished in subdued Scandinavian style. 89 rooms.

First Hotel Kong Frederik $$$ *Vester Voldgade 25, DK-1552 Copenhagen V; tel: 33 12 59 02;* www.firsthotels.com. Close to Rådhuspladsen and Tivoli. It retains the classic 'English' atmosphere both in public areas and in the bedrooms. Some overlook the internal atrium, while others spy on the busy street. 100 rooms.

First Hotel Mayfair $$–$$$ *Helgolandsgade 3, DK-1653 Copenhagen V; tel: 70 12 17 00;* www.firsthotels.com. This little gem offers a friendly atmosphere, cosy rooms and a very high standard of personal service. A continental breakfast, hot drinks, afternoon cakes and a light evening buffet are included in the price – very helpful to those on a budget. 203 rooms.

Good Morning City Copenhagen Star $$$ *Colbjørnsensgade 13, DK-1652 Copenhagen V; tel: 33 22 11 00;* https://ligula.se/da/goodmorninghotels/copenhagen-star. Situated in the cluster of streets on the other side of Central Station from Tivoli, with well-appointed rooms. A good breakfast buffet is included. 134 rooms.

Grand Hotel $$–$$$ *Vesterbrogade 9A, DK-1620 Copenhagen V; tel: 33 27 69 00;* www.grandhotel.dk. An attractive facade, dating from 1890, fronts a carefully modernised and tastefully decorated hotel. The Ristorante Frascati serves great Italian food at night. 161 rooms.

Imperial Hotel $$$ *Vester Farimagsgade 9, DK-1606 Copenhagen V; tel: 33 12 80 00;* www.imperialhotel.dk. In a good location next to Vesterport

Station, a few minutes' walk from Rådhuspladsen and Tivoli Gardens. Modern, well-appointed, with elegant rooms, fine restaurants and on-site parking. 304 rooms.

Nimb $$$$ *Tivoli, Bernstorffsgade 5, DK-1630 Copenhagen V; tel: 88 70 00 00*; http://hotel.nimb.dk. A romantic's dream, Nimb is in a Moorish-style palace, beautifully illuminated at night, inside Tivoli gardens. Its 38 fabulous boutique rooms contain a deeply satisfying blend of modern and antique furniture, and sleek bathrooms come with bathtubs. If you're here in winter, working fireplaces add to the romance.

Radisson Collection Royal Copenhagen Hotel $$$-$$$$ *Hammerichsgade 1, DK-1611 Copenhagen V; tel: 33426000*; www.radissoncollection. com. Dating from 1960, this iconic 20-storey hotel (designed, down to the cutlery and door knobs, by architect Arne Jacobsen) offers a panoramic view of Tivoli Gardens and the city. Rooms are in modern Danish style, although Room 606 retains its original 1960s decor. There's a rooftop restaurant, sauna and private parking. 261 rooms.

Scandic Palace Hotel $$$$ *Rådhuspladsen 57, DK-1550 Copenhagen V; tel: 33 14 40 50*; www.scandichotels.dk. An imposing historical landmark on Rådhuspladsen, the Palace has been carefully renovated and modernised and it now meets the highest standards. Superior rooms are worth paying extra for: ask for one on a higher floor with a balcony for good city views. 169 rooms.

Scandic Webers $$-$$$ *Vesterbrogade 11B, DK-1620 Copenhagen V; tel: 33 31 14 32*; www.scandichotels.dk. Scandic hotels offer business and leisure travellers reliably comfortable rooms and good facilities, and the Webers conforms to type. It has a trendy bar and peaceful courtyard, and guests have free access to the Scandic Copenhagen's gym/sauna. 152 rooms.

The Square $$$-$$$$ *Rådhuspladsen 14, DK-1550 Copenhagen V; tel: 33 38 12 00*; www.thesquare.dk. Right on Rådhuspladsen, this sleek design hotel offers several grades of rooms, smiling staff and a rooftop breakfast room with fine views. 268 rooms.

Wakeup Copenhagen $ *Carsten Niebuhrs Gade 11, DK-1577 Copenhagen V; tel: 44 80 00 00;* www.wakeupcopenhagen.com. This budget hotel has clean, modern, compact rooms with flatscreen TVs and free WiFi. Prices rise as you go higher up the building – the 'Wakeup Heaven' rooms on the top floor have the best views. The hotel represents good value in an expensive city. 510 rooms.

AROUND KONGENS NYTORV

Generator Hostel $ *Adelgade 5-7, Copenhagen 1304, tel: 78 79 37 01;* https://staygenerator.com. With prices starting from 125kr in a shared dormitory (although there are also single and double rooms with en-suite bathroom available for around 500kr), this is one of the cheapest options in Copenhagen. Its minimalistic Scandinavian interior is all about wood and homey feeling. Located within walking distance from the city centre, harbour and gardens, it boasts an amazing outdoor terrace, a café, and a travel shop where you can buy tickets for city tours.

Hotel d'Angleterre $$$$ *Kongens Nytorv 34, DK-1050 Copenhagen K; tel: 33 12 00 95;* www.dangleterre.com. Established more than 260 years ago, this five-star 'fairy-tale' hotel has traditionally provided a refuge for the rich and famous. Spa, indoor pool and a Michelin-starred restaurant. 92 rooms.

UNIVERSITY QUARTER AND PARKS

Ascot Hotel $$$ *Studiestræde 61, DK-1554 Copenhagen V; tel: 78 76 91 40;* www.ascot-hotel.dk. In a distinguished old bathhouse building in the Latin Quarter, this hotel is decorated with a mixture of antiques and modern furniture. 144 rooms.

Hotel Christian IV $$–$$$ *Dronningens Tværgade 45, DK-1302 Copenhagen K; tel: 33 32 10 44;* www.hotelchristianiv.dk. A small, highly pleasing hotel right by the lovely King's Garden. Rooms are neat and bright, and fitted with modern Danish furniture, and rates include a good breakfast spread. Quiet neighbourhood. 42 rooms.

Hotel Kong Arthur $$$$ *Nørre Søgade 11, DK-1370 Copenhagen V; tel: 33 11 12 12;* www.arthurhotels.dk. Established in 1882, and situated beside Peblinge Lake, this appealing hotel has retained much of its original charm. A popular choice with both Danish and foreign visitors, it has a friendly and thoroughly Danish atmosphere. 155 rooms.

Skt Petri Hotel $$$–$$$$ *Krystalgade 22, DK-1172 Copenhagen K; tel: 33 45 91 00;* www.sktpetri.com. This award-winning five-star design hotel shows great attention to detail, right down to the electronica music that its staff commission and pipe into the lifts. In summer, there is also an attractive outdoor area for drinks and dinner. 288 rooms, including 26 suites.

NYHAVN AND BEYOND

71 Nyhavn Hotel $$$–$$$$ *Nyhavn 71, DK-1051 Copenhagen K; tel: 33 43 62 00;* www.71nyhavnhotel.com. Delightfully located at the foot of Nyhavn in two well-renovated and carefully restored spice warehouses, this modern hotel has rather small rooms, a rustic atmosphere and great views over the harbour. 130 rooms.

Adina Apartment Hotel Copenhagen $$$$ *Amerikaplads 7, DK-2100 Copenhagen Ø; tel: 39 69 10 00;* www.tfehotels.com. These fabulous four-star hotel apartments are equipped with kitchenettes, a washer/drier, etc, and guests have access to a small gym, swimming pool and jacuzzi. Just north of the Little Mermaid and handy for the cruise-ship port. 126 studios and apartments.

Copenhagen Admiral Hotel $$$–$$$$ *Toldbodgade 24–28, DK-1253 Copenhagen K; tel: 33 74 14 14;* www.admiralhotel.dk. Standing beside the harbour, the hotel was formerly a granary constructed in 1787. Comfortably converted, it has retained the 200-year-old Pomeranian pine wooden beams in the rooms. Features its own well-regarded brasserie restaurant and a sauna. 366 rooms including 52 suites.

Copenhagen Strand $$$ *Havnegade 37, DK-1058 Copenhagen K; tel: 33 48 99 00;* www.copenhagenstrand.dk. This cosy hotel, with quaint maritime touches, is in a converted warehouse dating from 1869, on a side street just off Nyhavn. 174 rooms and suites.

Phoenix Copenhagen $$$ *Bredgade 37, DK-1260 Copenhagen K; tel: 33 95 95 00;* www.phoenixcopenhagen.dk. An elegant hotel close to the Royal Palace and Kongens Nytorv. All rooms and suites were fully renovated in 2018 and are air-conditioned. 213 rooms.

Scandic Front Hotel $$$$ *Sankt Annæ Plads 21, DK-1250 Copenhagen K; tel: 33 13 34 00;* www.scandichotels.com. This modern boutique hotel is on the harbour front close to Nyhavn. The rooms are sleek and well-equipped – the lovely split-level suites have face-on views of the Opera House. Underground parking. 132 rooms.

OUTLYING AREAS

Clarion Hotel Copenhagen Airport $$$–$$$$ *Ellehammersvej 20, DK-2770 Copenhagen; tel: 32 50 15 01;* www.nordicchoicehotels.com. This hotel offers Copenhagen's largest rooms, five-star luxury and a lobby filled with famous Arne Jacobsen chairs usually holding celebrities. You can't get closer to the airport – it's just two minutes' walk to Terminal 3. 383 rooms.

Radisson Blu Scandinavia Hotel $$–$$$ *Amager Boulevard 70, DK-2300 Copenhagen S; tel: 33 96 50 00;* www.radissonblu.com/scandinaviahotel-copenhagen. A 25-storey building that dominates the skyline 1km (half a mile) from Tivoli Gardens across the water on Amager. Rooms are furnished in standard Scandinavian decor, and most have fine views. Convenient for the airport. 544 rooms.

DICTIONARY

ENGLISH–DANISH

adj adjective   **adv** adverb   **BE** British English   **n** noun   **prep** preposition   **v** verb

A

a (with common nouns) en; **(with neuter nouns)** et
able kunne
about cirka
above ovenpå
accept v tage imod; **(approval)** godkende
access n adgang
accessory tilbehør
accident ulykke
account konto
ache smerte
acupuncture akupunktur
adapter adapter
address n adresse
admission adgang
admitted give adgang for
after efter
afternoon eftermiddag
aftershave lotion barbersprit
again igen
against mod
age alder
air conditioning klimaanlæg
air mattress luftmadras
airmail luftpost
airplane fly
airport lufthavn

aisle seat sæde ved midtergangen
alarm clock vækkeur
alcohol alkohol
alcoholic adj alkoholisk
allergic allergisk
allergic reaction allergisk reaktion
alphabet alfabet
also også
alter v ændre
altitude sickness bjergsyge
amazing forbløffende
amber rav
ambulance ambulance
American amerikaner
amethyst ametyst
amount n **(money)** beløb
amusement park forlystelsespark
analgesic smertestillende middel
and og
anesthetic narkose
animal dyr
ankle ankel
answer svar
antibiotic antibiotikum
antidepressant antidepressivt middel
antique antikvitet
antiques store antikvitetshandler

antiseptic cream antiseptisk creme
any nogen
anyone nogen
anything noget
anywhere hvor som helst
apartment lejlighed
aperitif aperitif
appendix blindtarm
appliance udstyr
appointment aftale
arcade spillehal
architect arkitekt
arm arm
aromatherapy aromaterapi
around (approximately) omkring; **(around the corner)** rundt om
arrival ankomst
arrive ankomme
art kunst
art gallery kunstgalleri
aspirin hovedpinepille
assistance hjælp
assorted blandet
asthma astma
astringent sammentrækkende middel
at ved
ATM pengeautomat
attack n overfald
attend deltage

attractive køn
audio guide lydguide
Australia Australien
average gennemsnitlig
away væk
awful skrækkelig

B

baby baby
baby bottle sutteflaske
baby food babymad
baby wipes vådservietter
babysitter babysitter
back ryg
backache rygsmerter
backpack rygsæk
bad dårlig
bag (purse) taske; **(shopping)** pose
baggage [BE] bagage
baggage check bagageopbevaring
baggage claim bagagebånd
bakery bageri
balance (finance) saldo
balcony altan
ballet ballet
bandage n plaster
bank (finance) bank
bank note seddel
bar bar
barber herrefrisør
basket kurv

basketball game basketballkamp

bath bad

bathing suit badedragt

bathrobe badekåbe

bathroom badeværelse

battery batteri

battleground kampplads

be være

beach ball badebold

beard skæg

beautiful smuk

beauty salon skønhedssalon

bed seng

before (time) før

begin begynde

behind bagved

beige beige

bell (electric) ringeklokke

below nedenunder

belt bælte

berth køje

better bedre

between mellem

bicycle cykel

big stor

bike route cykelsti

bikini bikini

bill (restaurant) regning; **(bank note)** seddel

binoculars kikkert

bird fugl

birth fødsel

birthday fødselsdag

black sort

bladder blære

blade barberblad

blanket tæppe

bleach blegning

bleed bløde

blind (window) rullegardin

blister blist

blocked stoppet

blood blod

blood pressure blodtryk

blouse bluse

blow dry føntørre

blue blå

boat båd

boat trip bådtur

body krop

bone knogle

book bog

booklet (of tickets) rabatkort

bookstore boghandel

boot støvle

boring kedelig

born født

botanical garden botanisk have

botany botanik

bother genere

bottle flaske

bottle opener oplukker

bottom forneden

bowel tarm

bowl skål

box æske

boxing match boksekamp

boy dreng

boyfriend kæreste

bra bh

bracelet armbånd

brake n bremse

break (out of order) være i uorden

breakdown (car) få motorstop

breakfast morgenmad

breast bryst

breathe trække vejret

bridge bro

bring tage med

bring down få ned

British (person) brite; adj britisk

broken i stykker

brooch broche

broom kost

brown brun

bruise blåt mærke

brush n børste

bucket spand

bug insekt

build bygge

building bygning

burn brandsår

bus bus

bus station busstation

bus stop busholdeplads

business card visitkort

business center (at hotel) businesscenter

business class business class

business district forretningskvarter

business trip forretningsrejse

busy optaget

but men

butane gas flaskegas

butcher slagter

button knap

buy købe

C

cabin (ship) kahyt

cafe café

calculator regnemaskine

calendar kalender

call n (phone) opringning; v ringe; **(summon)** ringe efter

calm rolig

camera kamera

camera case fototaske

camera shop fotoforretning

camp bed campingseng

camp v campere

camping camping

camping equipment campingudstyr

campsite campingplads

can opener dåseåbner

can v **(be able to)** kan; n **(container)** dåse

Canada Canada

Canadian canadier

cancel annullere

candle stearinlys

candy store slikbutik

cap kasket

car bil

car hire [BE] biludlejning

car mechanic bilmekaniker

car park [BE] parkeringsplads

car rental biludlejning

car seat barnesæde

carafe karaffel

card kort

card game kortspil

cardigan cardigan

carry bære

cart indkøbsvogn

carton (of cigarettes) karton

case (camera) taske

cash v Indløse; n kontant

cashier kasse

casino kasino

castle slot; borg

caution forsigtig

cave hule

CD cd
cell phone mobiltelefon
cemetery kirkegård
center of town centrum
centimeter centimeter
ceramics keramik
certain vis
certificate attest
chair stol
change n (money) byttepenge; v (money) veksle; v (clothes, diaper) skifte
charcoal trækul
charge n gebyr; v koste
cheap billig
check (restaurant) n regning; (banking) check; v (someone, something) kontrollere; (luggage) tjekke ind
check-in desk (airport) check-in skranke
checking account checkkonto
check out v tjekke ud
check-up (medical) undersøgelse
cheers skål
chef køkkenchef
chemical toilet kemisk toilet
chemist [BE] apotek
cheque [BE] check
chess skak
chess set skakspil
chest brystkasse
chest pain smerter i brystet
child barn
child's seat barnesæde
children's clothing børnetøj

children's portion børneportion
choice valg
church kirke
cigar cigar
cigarette cigaret
cinema [BE] biograf
classical klassisk
clean adj ren; v gøre rent
cleansing cream rensecreme
clear v slette
cliff klippe
clip clips
clock ur
close v lukke
closed lukket
cloth stof
clothing tøj
clothing store tøjbutik
cloud sky
coat n (clothing) frakke
coin mønt
cold (illness) forkølelse; adj kold
collar flip
colleague kollega
color farve
comb kam
come komme
comedy lystspil
commission (fee) kommission
common (frequent) almindelig
compartment (train) kupé
compass kompas
complaint klage
computer computer; pc
concert koncert
concert hall koncertsal
condom kondom
conference room mødelokale

confirm bekræfte
confirmation bekræftelse
congratulations til lykke
connect v koble sig på
connection (transportation, internet) forbindelse
constipation forstoppelse
consulate konsulat
contact lens kontaktlinse
contagious smitsom
contain indeholde
contraceptive præventivmiddel
contract kontrakt
control kontrol
convention hall konferencesal
cooking facilities køkkenfaciliteter
copper kobber
corkscrew proptrækker
corner hjørne
cost n omkostning; v koste
cot klapseng
cotton bomuld
cough n hoste
counter disk
country land
countryside på landet
court house retsbygning
cover charge beregning per kuvert
cramps krampe
crayon farveblyant
cream (toiletry) creme
credit kredit
credit card kreditkort

crib barneseng
crockery [BE] spisestel
cross-country skiing langrend
crossing (maritime) overfart
crossroads vejkryds
crown (Danish currency) krone
crystal krystal
cufflink manchetknap
cuisine køkken
cup kop
currency valuta
currency exchange office vekselkontor
current (ocean) strøm
curtain gardin
customs told
customs declaration form toldangivelsesformular
cut n (wound) snitsår; v (with scissors) klippe
cut glass slebet glas
cycling race cykelløb

D

dairy mejeri
damaged beskadiget
dance club diskotek
dance n dans; v danse
danger fare
dangerous farlig
Danish (person) dansker; adj dansk
dark mørk
date (appointment) stævnemøde; (day) dato
day dag
decision beslutning
deck (ship) dæk

deck chair liggestol
declare (customs) fortolde
deep dyb
degree (temperature) grad
delay forsinkelse
delicatessen delikatesseforretning
delicious dejlig
deliver levere
delivery levering
denim denim
Denmark Danmark
dentist tandlæge
denture protese
deodorant deodorant
depart afgå
department (shop) afdeling
department store stormagasin
departure afgang
departure gate afgangsgate
deposit n (bank) indskud; (down payment) depositum
dessert dessert
detergent opvaskemiddel
detour (traffic) omkørsel
diabetic diabetiker
diamond diamant
diaper ble
diarrhea diarré
dictionary ordbog
diesel diesel
diet kost
difficult svær
digital digital
dining car spisevogn
dining room spisesalen

dinner middag
direct adj direkte; v (someone) vise vej til
direction vejangivelse
directory (phone) telefonbog
dirty beskidt
disabled handicappet
disc (parking) parkeringsskive
disconnect v (computer) koble sig fra
discount rabat
disease sygdom
dish (food item) ret
dishes (plates) spisetallerkner
dishwasher opvaskemaskine
dishwashing detergent opvaskemiddel
disinfectant desinficeringsmiddel
display case udstillingsmontre
district (of town) kvarter
disturb forstyrre
divorced skilt
dizzy svimmel
doctor læge
doctor's office lægekonsultation
dog hund
doll dukke
dollar (U.S.) dollar
domestic (airport terminal) indenrigs
domestic flight indenrigsfly
double bed dobbeltseng
double room dobbeltværelse
down ned

downtown area indre by
dozen dusin
dress n kjole
drink n drikkevare; (cocktail) drink; v drikke
drinking water drikkevand
drip dryppe
drive køre
driver's license kørekort
drop (liquid) dråbe
drugstore apotek
dry tør
dry cleaner renseri
dummy [BE] (baby's) sut
during i løbet af
duty (customs) told
duty-free goods toldfri varer
duty-free shop toldfri butik
dye farvning

E

each hver
ear øre
ear drops øredråber
earache ondt i ørerne
early tidligt
earring ørenring
east øst
easy nem
eat spise
economy class økonomiklasse
elastic elastik
electric elektrisk
electrical outlet stikkontakt
electricity elektricitet
electronic elektronisk
elevator elevator

e-mail e-mail
e-mail address e-mail-adresse
embassy ambassade
embroidery broderi
emerald smaragd
emergency nødstilfælde
emergency exit nødudgang
empty tom
enamel emalje
end slutning
engaged (phone) optaget
England England
English (language) engelsk; (person) englænder
enjoyable dejlig
enlarge forstørre
enough nok
enter v indtaste
entrance indgang
entrance fee entré
entry (access) adgang
envelope konvolut
equipment udstyr
eraser viskelæder
escalator rulletrappe
estimate n overslag; (quotation) tilbud
e-ticket e-billet
e-ticket check-in e-billet check-in
eurocheque eurocheck
Europe Europa
European Union Europæiske Fællesskab
evening aften
every hver
everything alt
exchange rate vekselkurs

exchange v (money) veksle
excursion udflugt
excuse v undskylde
exhibition udstilling
exit n udgang; v (computer) forlade
expect vente
expense udgift
expensive dyr
express ekspres
expression udtryk
extension (phone) lokal
extra ekstra
eye øje
eye drops øjendråber
eye shadow øjenskygge
eyesight syn

F

fabric (cloth) stof
face ansigt
facial ansigtsbehandling
factory fabrik
fair messe
fall v falde
family familie
fan ventilator
far langt
fare (ticket) billet
farm bondegård
far-sighted langsynet
fast adj hurtig
fast-food place burgerbar
faucet vandhane
fax fax
fax number faxnummer
fee (commission) kommission
feed v made
feel (physical state) føle
ferry færge

fever feber
few et par stykker
field mark
file (for nails) fil
fill in (form) udfylde
filling (tooth) plombe
film [BE] film
filter filter
find v finde
fine (OK) fint
fine arts kunst
finger finger
fire brand
fire door branddør
fire escape brandtrappe
fire exit nødudgang
first første
first-aid kit nødhjælpskasse
first class første klasse
first course forret
fishing fiskeri
fit v passe
fitting room prøverum
fix v reparere
flashlight lommelygte
flat [BE] (apartment) lejlighed
flatware bestik
flea market loppemarked
flight fly
floor etage
florist blomsterhandler
flower blomst
flu influenza
fluid væske
fog tåge
follow følge
food mad
food poisoning madforgiftning
foot fod
football [BE] fodbold

for for
forbidden forbudt
forecast vejrudsigt
foreign udenlandsk
forest skov
forget glemme
fork gaffel
form (document) formular
fountain springvand
frame (glasses) stel
free ledigt
freezer fryser
fresh frisk
friend ven
from fra
frost frostvejr
frying pan stegepande
full fuld
full-time fuldtids
furniture møbel

G

gallery galleri
game spil
garage garage
garbage skrald
garden have
gas benzin
gasoline benzin
gauze gaze
gem ædelsten
general almindelig
general delivery poste restante
general practitioner [BE] praktiserende læge
genuine ægte
get (find) komme til
get off stige af
get up stå op
gift gave
gift shop gavebutik

girl pige
girlfriend kæreste
give give
gland kirtel
glass (drinking) glas
glasses (optical) briller
glove handske
glue lim
go away gå væk
go back køre tilbage
go out gå ud
gold guld
golf club golfkølle
golf course golfbane
golf tournament golfturnering
good god
good afternoon goddag
good evening godaften
good morning godmorgen
good night godnat
goodbye farvel
gram gram
grandchild barnebarn
gray grå
great (excellent) storartet
Great Britain Storbritannien
green grøn
greengrocer's [BE] grønthandler
greeting hilsen
ground-floor room [BE] værelse i stueetagen
groundsheet teltunderlag
group gruppe
guesthouse pensionat
guide dog førerhund
guide n guide
guidebook rejsefører
gym motionscenter

gynecologist gynækolog

H

hair hår
hair dryer hårtørrer
hairbrush hårbørste
haircut klipning
hairdresser frisør
hairspray hårlak
hall (room) sal
hammer hammer
hammock hængekøje
hand hånd
hand cream håndcreme
hand washable vaske
  i hånden
handbag [BE] håndtaske
handicrafts kunsthåndværk
handkerchief lom-
  metørklæde
handmade håndlavet
hanger bøjle
happy glad
harbor havn
hard hård
hardware store
  isenkræmmer
hare hare
hat hat
have (must) skulle;
  (possess) have
hay fever høfeber
head hoved
headache hovedpine
headlight billygte
headphones hoved-
  telefon
health food store
  helsekostforretning
health insurance
  sygeforsikring
hearing-impaired
  hørehæmmet

heart hjerte
heart attack hjerte-
  anfald
heat v opvarme
heating varme
heavy tung
hello hej
helmet hjelm
help hjælp; **(oneself)**
  tage selv
here her
hi hej
high adj høj
high tide flod
highchair høj stol
highway motorvej
hill bakke
hire [BE] v leje
history historie
hole hul
holiday helligdag;
  [BE] ferie
home hjem
horseback riding
  ridning
hospital hospital
hot (temperature) varm
hotel hotel
hotel directory
  hotelfortegnelse
hotel reservation
  værelsesbestilling
hour (time) time
house hus
how hvordan
how far hvor langt
how long hvor længe
how many hvor mange
how much hvor meget
hug v kramme
hungry sulten
hunting jagt
hurry travlt
hurt gøre ondt

husband mand

I

I jeg
ice is
icy (weather) iskoldt
identification (card)
  id-kort
if hvis
ill [BE] syg
illness sygdom
important vigtig
imported importeret
impressive imponerende
in i
include iberegne
indoor indendørs
inexpensive billig
infected betændt
infection betændelse
inflammation
  betændelse
information information
information desk
  informationsluge
injection indsprøjtning
injure komme til skade
injury kvæstelse
inn kro
innocent uskyldig
inquiry forespørgsel
insect bite insektbid
insect repellent
  insekt-spray
insect spray insekt-
  spray
inside indenfor
instant messenger
  instant messenger
insurance forsikring
insurance claim
  forsikringskrav
interest (finance) rente
interested interesseret

interesting interessant
international
  international; **(airport
  terminal)** udenrigs
international flight
  udenrigsfly
internet internet
internet cafe inter-
  netcafé
interpreter tolk
intersection vejkryds
introduce præsentere
introduction (social)
  præsentation
investment investering
invitation indbydelse
invite v indbyde
invoice faktura
iodine jod
Ireland Irland
Irish (person) irlænder,
  adj irsk
iron n **(clothing)**
  strygejern; v stryge
itemized bill udspecificeret regning

J

jacket jakke
jar (container) glas
jaw kæbe
jazz jazz
jeans cowboybukser
jet ski jetski
jeweler guldsmed
join v komme med
joint (anatomy) led
journey rejse
just (only) bare

K

keep beholde
kerosene petroleum
key nøgle

key card nøglekort
kiddie pool børnebassin
kidney nyre
kilogram kilogram
kilometer kilometer
kind *adj* rar; *n* slags
kiss *v* kysse
knee knæ
knife kniv
knitwear strikvarer
knock banke på
know vide

L

label etiket
lace blonde
lactose intolerant
 laktoseintolerant
lake sø
lamp lampe
landscape landskab
language sprog
lantern lygte
large stor
last sidst
late (time) sent;
 (delay) forsinket
laugh grine
launderette [BE]
 møntvaskeri
laundromat møntvaskeri
laundry vasketøj
laundry facilities
 vaskerum
laundry service vaskeri
lawyer advokat
laxative afføringsmiddel
leather læder
leave *v* afgå; **(behind)**
 efterlade
left til venstre
left-luggage office
 [BE] bagageopbev-
 aring

leg ben
lens (camera) objektiv;
 (glasses) linse
less mindre
lesson undervisning
letter brev
library bibliotek
license (driving)
 kørekort
life boat redningsbåd
life guard (beach)
 livredder
life jacket redningsvest
life preserver redn-
 ingsbælte
lift [BE] elevator
light (color) lys;
 (weight) let
light bulb pære
lighter lighter
lightning lyn
like vil gerne; **(please)**
 kan lide
linen lærred
lip læbe
lipstick læbestift
liquor store vinhandel
listen høre på
liter liter
little (amount) en
 smule
live *v* bo
loafers hyttesko
local lokal
log off logge af
log on logge på
login log ind
long lange
long-sighted [BE]
 langsynet
look *v* se
lose miste
loss tab
lost faret vild

lost and found hit-
 tegodskontor
lost property office
 [BE] hittegodskontor
lotion lotion
loud (voice) høj
love *v* elske
lovely dejlig
low lav
low tide ebbe
luck lykke
luggage bagage
luggage cart baga-
 gevogn
luggage locker
 bagageboks
lunch frokost
lung lunge

M

magazine blad
magnificent storartet
maid stuepige
mail *n* post; *v* poste
mailbox postkasse
make-up *n* sminke
mall butikscenter
mallet kølle
man mand
manager direktør
manicure manicure
many mange
map kort
market *n* market
married gift
mass (religious
 service) messe
massage massage
match *n* **(sport)** kamp
material stof
matinée eftermid-
 dagsforestilling
mattress madras
may *v* må

meadow eng
meal måltid
mean *v* betyde
measure tage mål af
measuring cup
 målekrus
measuring spoon
 måleske
mechanic mekaniker
medicine (drug)
 medicin
meet mødes
memorial mindesmærke
memory card hukom-
 melseskort
mend reparere
menu menu; menukort
message besked
meter meter
middle midten
midnight midnat
mileage kilometerpenge
minute minut
mirror spejl
miscellaneous
 forskellig
Miss frøken
miss *v* **(lacking)** mangle
mistake fejltagelse
mobile phone [BE]
 mobiltelefon
moisturizing cream
 fugtighedscreme
moment øjeblik
money penge
money order postan-
 visning
month måned
monument monument
moon måne
mop *n* moppe
moped knallert
more mere
morning morgen

mosque moské
mosquito net myggenet
motel motel
motorboat motorbåd
motorcycle motorcykel
motorway [BE] motorvej
moustache overskæg
mouth mund
mouthwash mundvand
move v flytte
movie film
Mr. hr.
Mrs. fru
much meget
mug n krus
mugging overfald
muscle muskel
museum museum
music musik
musical musical
must (have to) måtte

N

nail (body) negl
nail clippers negle-
  klipper
nail file neglefil
nail salon neglesalon
name navn
napkin serviet
nappy [BE] ble
narrow smal
nationality nationalitet
natural naturlig
nausea kvalme
near nær
nearby i nærheden
near-sighted nærsynet
neck hals
necklace halskæde
need v brug for
needle nål
nerve nerve
never aldrig

new ny
newspaper avis
newsstand aviskiosk
next næste
next to ved siden af
nice (beautiful) dejlig
night nat
no nej
noisy støjende
none ingen
non-smoking ikke-ryger
noon middag
normal normal
north nord
nose næse
not ikke
note (bank note) seddel
notebook notesbog
nothing ikke noget
notice (sign) skilt
notify underrette
novice begynderniveau
now nu
number nummer
nurse sygeplejerske

O

o'clock klokken
occupation stilling
occupied optaget
office kontor
off-licence [BE]
  vinhandel
oil spiseolie
old gammel
old town gamle bydel
on på
on time til tiden
once en gang
one-way ticket
  enkeltbillet
only kun
open adj åben; v åbne
opera opera

operation operation
operator telefonist
opposite overfor
optician optiker
or eller
orange (color) orange
orchestra orkester;
  (seats) parket
order n bestilling; v
  bestille
out of order virker ikke
out of stock udsolgt
outlet (electric) stik-
  kontakt
outside udenfor
oval oval
overlook n udkigspost
oxygen treatment
  oxygenbehandling

P

pacifier (baby's) sut
packet pakke
pad (sanitary)
  hygiejnebind
pail spand
pain smerte
painkiller smertes-
  tillende middel
paint n maling; v male
painting maleri
pair par
pajamas pyjamas
palace slot
palpitations hjerte-
  banken
pants bukser
panty hose strømpe-
  bukser
paper papir
paper towel papirhånd-
  klæde
parcel [BE] pakke
parents forældre

park n park; v parkere
parking parkering
parking disc parker-
  ingsskive
parking garage
  parkeringskælder
parking lot parkering-
  splads
parking meter
  parkometer
part del
part-time deltid
party (social gather-
  ing) fest
passport pas
passport control
  paskontrol
passport photo pasfoto
paste (glue) klister
pastry shop konditori
patch lappe
path sti
patient patient
pattern mønster
pay betale
payment betaling
peak n (mountain)
  bjergtop
pearl perle
pedestrian fodgænger
pediatrician børnelæge
pedicure pedicure
peg (tent) pløk
pen pen; kuglepen
pencil blyant
pendant vedhæng
penicillin penicillin
per day per dag
per hour per time
per person per person
per week per uge
percentage procentsats
perfume parfume
perhaps måske

period (monthly) menstruation
permit n (fishing) fiskekort; (hunting) jagtkort
person person
personal personlig
petite petit
petrol [BE] benzin
pewter tinlegering
pharmacy apotek
phone card telefonkort
photo billede
photocopy n fotokopi
photograph n billede
photography fotografering
phrase vending
pick up v (go get) hente
picnic medbragt mad
picnic basket madkurv
piece stykke
pill pille
pillow pude
PIN pinkode
pin n (brooch) nål
pink lyserød
pipe pibe
place n sted
plane fly
planetarium planetarium
plaster [BE] (bandage) plaster
plastic plastic
plastic bag plasticpose
plastic wrap plastikfolie
plate tallerken
platform [BE] (station) perron
platinum platin
play n (theatre) stykke; v spille
playground legeplads

playpen kravlegård
please vær venlig
plug (electric) stik
plunger svuppert; vaskesuger
pneumonia lungebetændelse
pocket lomme
point of interest seværdighed
point v pege
poison gift
poisoning forgiftning
pole (ski) skistav; (tent) teltstang
police politi
police report politianmeldelse
police station politistation
pond dam
pool svømmebassin
porcelain porcelæn
port havn
portable transportabel
porter portier
portion portion
post [BE] n post; v poste
post office posthus
postage porto
postage stamp frimærke
postcard postkort
pot gryde
pottery pottemageri
pound (British currency, weight) pund
powder pudder
pregnant gravid
premium (gas) 98 oktan
prescribe skrive recept på
prescription recept
present n gave

press (iron) presse
pressure tryk
pretty køn
price pris
price-fixed menu dagens menu
print n (photo) aftryk; v (document) udskrive
private privat
profit n overskud
program (of events) program
pronounce v udtale
pronunciation n udtale
provide skaffe
pull v trække
pump pumpe
puncture punktering
purchase n køb; v købe
pure ren
purple violet
purse (handbag) håndtaske
push v skubbe
pushchair [BE] klapvogn
put sætte

Q

quality kvalitet
quantity mængde
question n spørgsmål
quick hurtig
quiet stille

R

race væddeløb
race track væddeløbsbane
racket (sport) ketsjer
radio radio
railway station [BE] jernbanestation
rain regnvejr

raincoat regnfrakke
rape n voldtægt
rash udslet
rate n (exchange) vekselkurs; (price) takst
razor barbermaskine
razor blade barberblad
ready færdig
real (genuine) ægte
rear bagerst
receipt kvittering
reception reception
receptionist receptionist
recommend anbefale
rectangular rektangulær
red rød
reduction rabat
refrigerator køleskab
refund v få pengene tilbage
regards hilsner
region område
registered mail anbefalet
registration indskrivning
regular (gas) 95 oktan
relationship forhold
reliable pålidelig
religion religion
rent v leje
rental udlejning
rental car udlejningsbil
repair n reparation; v reparere
repeat v gentage
report (theft) anmelde
request n anmodning; v anmode
required nødvendig
requirement forespørgsel
reservation reservation

reservations office
pladsreserveringen
reserve bestille
reserved reserveret
rest *n* rest
restaurant restaurant
restroom toilet
retired pensioneret
return (come back)
komme tilbage; (give
back) returnere
return ticket [BE]
returbillet
rib ribben
ribbon bånd
right (correct) rigtigt;
(direction) til højre
ring (jewelry) ring;
(bell) ringe på
river flod
road vej
road assistance hjælp
på vejen
road map vejkort
road sign vejskilt
robbery tyveri
romantic romantisk
room (hotel) værelse;
(space) plads
room number værelses-
nummer
room service room-
service; service på
værelset
room temperature
rumtemperatur
rope reb
round rund
round (golf) runde
round-trip ticket
returbillet
route rute
rowboat robåd
rubber (material)

gummi
rubbish [BE] skrald
ruby rubin

S

safe n (vault) boks;
(not in danger)
sikker
safety pin sikkerhedsnål
sailboat sejlbåd
sale *n* salg; (bargains)
udsalg
same samme
sand sand
sandal sandal
sanitary napkin
hygiejnebind
sapphire safir
satin satin
saucepan kasserolle
saucer underkop
sauna sauna
save *v* gemme
savings account
opsparingskonto
scarf tørklæde
scenery landskab
scenic route køn rute
school skole
scissors saks
scooter scooter
Scotland Skotland
screwdriver skruetræk-
ker
sculpture skulptur
sea hav
season sæson
seat plads
seat belt sele
second sekund
second class anden
klasse
second-hand shop
marskandiser;

genbrugsbutik
section afdeling
see se
sell sælge
send sende
senior citizen pensionist
sentence sætning
separated (relation-
ship) separeret
serious alvorlig
serve (meal) servere
service (restaurant)
betjening
set menu fast menu
sew sy
shampoo shampoo
shape form
sharp (pain) skarp
shave *n* barbering
shaving brush
barberbørste
shaving cream
barbercreme
shelf hylde
ship *n* skib; *v* forsende
shirt skjorte
shoe sko
shoe store skoforretning
shop *n* butik
shopping indkøb
shopping area indkøb-
scenter
shopping centre [BE]
butikscenter
shopping mall
butikscenter
short kort
shorts shorts
short-sighted [BE]
kortsynet
shoulder skulder
shovel *n* skovl
show *n* show; *v* vise
shower (stall) bruser

shrine helgengrav
shut lukket
shutter (window)
skodde
side side
sightseeing sightseeing
sightseeing tour
rundtur
sign underskrive
sign (notice) skilt;
v underskrive
signature underskrift
silk silke
silver sølv
silverware sølvtøj
since siden
sing synge
single *n* (ticket)
enkeltbillet; (unmar-
ried) ugift
single room enkelt-
værelse
size størrelse; (clothes)
mål; (shoes) nummer
skate *v* skøjte
skating rink skøjtebane
skin hud
skirt nederdel
sky himmel
sleep *v* sove
sleeping bag sovepose
sleeping car sovevogn
sleeping pill sovepille
sleeve ærme
slice *n* skive
slide (photo) dias
slipper hjemmesko
slow langsom
small lille
smoke ryge
smoker ryger
snack mellemmåltid
snack bar snackbar
sneaker gummisko

snorkeling equipment snorkeludstyr

snow sne

soap sæbe

soccer fodbold

soccer match fodboldkamp

sock sok

socket (electric) stikkontakt

soft blød

sold out udsolgt

someone nogen

something noget

song sang

soon snart

sore (painful) øm

sore throat ondt i halsen

sorry beklager

sort (kind) slags

south syd

souvenir souvenir

souvenir shop souvenirbutik

spa spa

spatula spatel

speak v tale

special særlig

specialist specialist

speciality specialitet

spell v stave

spend bruge

spine rygrad

sponge svamp

spoon ske

sport sport

sporting goods store sportsforretning

sprained forstuvet

square (shape) firkantet

stadium stadium

staff personale

stain plet

stainless steel rustfrit stål

stairs trappe

stamp n (postage) frimærke; v (ticket) stemple

staple hæfteklamme

star stjerne

start begynde

starter [BE] (meal) forret

stationery store papirhandel

stay (trip) ophold; v (remain) blive; v (reside) bo

steal stjæle

sterling silver sterlingsølv

sting n stik; v stikke

stockings strømpe

stomach mave

stomachache mavepine

stop (bus) busholdeplads; v stop

store (shop) forretning

store directory butiksoversigt

stove ovn

straight ahead ligeud

strange underlig

street gade

street map gadekort

string snor

stroller klapvogn

strong stærk

student studerende

study v studere

stunning fantastisk flot

sturdy solid

subway metro

subway map togkort

suit (man's) habit; (woman's) dragt

suitcase kuffert

sun sol

sunburn solforbrænding

sunglasses solbriller

sunstroke solstik

sun-tan lotion solcreme

super (gas) 98 oktan

supermarket supermarked

supplement n tillæg

suppository stikpille

surgery [BE] lægekonsultation

surname efternavn

swallow sluge

sweater sweater

sweatshirt sweatshirt

sweet sød

swell hæve

swelling hævelse

swim v svømme

swimming svømning

swimming pool svømmebasin

swimming trunks badebukser

swollen hævet

symbol symbol

synagogue synagoge

synthetic syntetisk

system system

T

table bord

tablet (medical) pille

tailor skrædder

take tage

take away v [BE] tage med

taken (occupied) taget

tampon tampon

tap (water) vandhane

tax skat

taxi taxa

taxi rank [BE] taxaholdeplads

taxi stand taxaholdeplads

team hold

tear v rive i stykker

teaspoon teske

telephone booth telefonboks

telephone directory telefonbog

telephone n telefon; v ringe

telephone number telefonnummer

tell sige

temperature temperatur

temple tempel

temporary midlertidig

tennis court tennisbane

tennis match tenniskamp

tennis racket tennisketsjer

tent telt

tent peg teltpløk

tent pole teltstang

terminal terminal

terrace terrasse

terrible frygtelig

terrifying skrækindjagende

thank takke

thank you tak

theater teater

theft tyveri

then så

there der

thermometer termometer

thief tyv

thigh lår
thin tynd
think (believe) tro
thirsty tørstig
thread tråd
throat hals
through gennem
thumb tommelfinger
thunder torden
thunderstorm tordenvejr
ticket billet
ticket office billetluge
tide ebbe
tie slips
tie clip slipseklemme
time n tid; (recurrent occasion) gang
timetable [BE] køreplan
tin [BE] (container) dåse
tin opener [BE] dåseåbner
tire dæk
tired træt
tissue papirslommetørklæde
to til
tobacco tobak
tobacconist tobakshandler
today i dag
toe tå
toilet [BE] toilet
toilet paper toiletpapir
toiletry toiletartikel
tomb gravsted
tomorrow i morgen
tongue tunge
tonight i aften
too (also) også
too much for meget
tool værktøj
tooth tand
toothache tandpine

toothbrush tandbørste
toothpaste tandpasta
torn (clothes) gået i stykker
touch v røre
tour tur
tourist office turistkontor
tow truck kranbil
towards mod
towel håndklæde
tower tårn
town by
town hall rådhus
toy legetøj
toy store legetøjsforretning
track (train) spor
traffic light trafiklys
trail gangsti
trailer campingvogn
train tog
tram sporvogn
tranquillizer beroligende middel
transfer (money) overførsel
translate oversætte
travel rejse
travel agency rejsebureau
travel guide rejsefører
travel sickness køresyge
traveler's check rejsecheck
treatment behandling
tree træ
trim studsning
trip rejse
trolley bagagevogn
trousers [BE] bukser
T-shirt T-shirt
tube tube

turn (change direction) drej til
turtleneck højhalset
TV fjernsyn
tweezers pincet

U

ugly grim
umbrella paraply; (beach) parasol
unconscious bevidstløs
under under
underground station [BE] metrostation
underpants underbukser
undershirt undertrøje
understand forstå
undress tage tøjet af
United States USA
university universitet
unleaded (fuel) blyfri
until indtil
up op
upstairs ovenpå
urgent haster
use brug
usually normalt

V

vacancy ledigt værelse
vacant ledig
vacation ferie
vaccinate vaccinere
vacuum cleaner støvsuger
valley dal
value værdi
value-added tax [BE] moms
vegetarian vegetar
vein vene
very meget
veterinarian dyrlæge
video camera

videokamera
view (panorama) udsigt
village landsby
visit n besøg; v besøge
visiting hours besøgstid
visually impaired synshæmmet
V-neck V-hals
volleyball game volleyballkamp
voltage spænding
vomit v kaste op

W

wait v vente
waiter tjener
waiting room venteværelse
waitress kvindelig tjener
wake vække
wake-up call morgenvækning
Wales Wales
walk n gåtur
wall mur
wallet tegnebog
want vil have
warm (temperature) varm; v (reheat) opvarme
wash vaske
washing machine vaskemaskine
watch n ur
water vand
waterfall vandfald
waterproof vandtæt
water-ski vandski
wave n bølge
way vej
weather vejr
weather forecast vejrudsigt
week uge

weekend weekend
well godt
west vest
what hvad
wheel hjul
wheelchair kørestol
when hvornår
where hvor
which hvilken
white hvid
who hvem
whole hele
why hvorfor
wide brede
widow (female) enke;
(male) enkemand
wife kone
wind vind
window vindue; (shop) butiksvindue
window seat vinduessæde
windsurfer windsurfer
wine list vinliste
wireless trådløs
wish v ønske
with med
withdraw (banking) få udbetalt
without uden
woman kvinde
wonderful vidunderlig
wood skov
wool uld
word ord
work v virke
worse værre
wound sår
write skrive
wrong forkert

X
X-ray røntgenfotografere

Y
year år
yellow gul
yes ja
yesterday i går
yet endnu
young ung
youth hostel van-drehjem

Z
zipper lynlås
zoo zoologisk have

DANISH–ENGLISH

A
adapter adapter
adgang n access; admission; entry
adresse n address
advokat lawyer
afdeling n department (shop); section; entry
afføringsmiddel laxative
afgang departure
afgangsgate departure gate
afgå depart; leave
aftale appointment
aften evening
aftryk n print (photo)
akupunktur acupuncture
alder age
aldrig never
alfabet alphabet
alkohol alcohol
allergisk allergic

allergisk reaktion allergic reaction
almindelig common (frequent); general
alt everything
altan balcony
alvorlig serious
ambassade embassy
ambulance ambulance
amerikaner American
ametyst amethyst
anbefale recommend
anbefalet registered mail
anden klasse second class
ankel ankle
ankomme arrive
ankomst arrival
anmelde report (theft)
anmodning n request
annullere cancel
ansigt face

ansigtsbehandling facial
antibiotikum antibiotic
antidepressivt middel antidepressant
antikvitet antique
antikvitetshandler antiques store
antiseptisk creme antiseptic cream
apotek pharmacy [chemist BE]
arkitekt architect
arm arm
armbånd bracelet
aromaterapi aroma-therapy
astma asthma
attest certificate
Australien Australia
automatgear automatic (car)
avis newspaper

aviskiosk newsstand

B
baby baby
babymad baby food
babysitter babysitter
bad bath
badebukser swimming trunks
badedragt bathing suit
badekåbe bathrobe
badeværelse bathroom
bagage luggage [baggage BE]
bagageboks luggage locker
bagagebånd baggage claim
bagageopbevaring baggage check
bagagevogn luggage cart [trolley BE]
bageri bakery

bagerst rear
bagved behind
bakke hill
ballet ballet
bane train
bank bank (finance)
banke på knock
bar bar
barberblad razor blade
barberbørste shaving brush
barbercreme shaving cream
barbering *n* shave
barbermaskine razor
barbersprit aftershave lotion
bare just (only)
barn child
barnebarn grandchild
barneseng crib
barnesæde car seat; child's seat
basketballkamp basketball game
batteri battery
bedre better
begynde begin; start
behandling treatment
beholde keep
beige beige
beklager sorry
bekræfte confirm
bekræftelse confirmation
beløb *n* amount (money)
ben leg
benzin gas [petrol BE]
beregning per kuvert cover charge
beroligende middel tranquillizer
beskadiget damaged
besked message

beskidt dirty
beslutning decision
bestik flatware
bestille *v* reserve; order
bestilling *n* order
besøg *n* visit
besøgstid visiting hours
betale pay
betaling payment
betjening service (restaurant)
betyde *v* mean
betændelse infection; inflammation
betændt infected
bevidstløs unconscious
bh bra
bibliotek library
bikini bikini
bil car
billede photo
billet ticket
billetluge ticket office
billig cheap
bilmekaniker car mechanic
biludlejning car rental [hire BE]
biograf movie theater [cinema BE]
bjergtop *n* peak (mountain)
blad magazine
blandet assorted
ble diaper [nappy BE]
blegning bleach
blindtarm appendix
blist blister
blod blood
blodtryk blood pressure
blomst flower
blomsterhandler florist
blonde lace
bluse blouse

blyant pencil
blyfri unleaded (fuel)
blød soft
bløde bleed
blå blue
blåt mærke bruise
bo *v* live
bog book
boghandel bookstore
boksekamp boxing match
bomuld cotton
bondegård farm
bord table
borg castle
botanisk have botanical garden
brand fire
branddør fire door
brandsår burn
brandtrappe fire escape
brede wide
bremse *n* brake
brev letter
briller glasses (optical)
brite British
bro bridge
broche brooch
broderi embroidery
brug use
brug for *v* need
bruge spend
brun brown
bruser *n* shower (stall)
bryst breast
brystkasse chest
bukser pants [trousers BE]
burgerbar fast-food place
bus bus
busholdeplads bus stop
business class business class

businesscenter business center (at hotel)
busstation bus station
butik *n* shop
butikscenter shopping mall [centre BE]
butiksoversigt store directory
by town
bygge build
bygning building
byttepenge *n* change (money)
bælte belt
bære carry
bøjle hanger
bølge *n* wave
børnebassin kiddie [paddling BE] pool
børnelæge pediatrician
børnemenu children's menu
børneportion children's portion
børnetøj children's clothing
børste *n* brush
båd boat
bådtur boat trip
bånd ribbon

C

café cafe
campere *v* camp
camping camping
campingplads campsite
campingseng camp bed
campingvogn trailer
Canada Canada
canadier Canadian
cardigan cardigan
cd CD

centimeter centimeter
centrum downtown area [centre BE]
check check [cheque BE] (banking)
check-in skranke check-in desk (airport)
checkkonto checking account
chokoladeforretning candy store
cigar cigar
cigaret cigarette
cirka about
clips clip
cowboybukser jeans
creme cream (toiletry)
cykel bicycle
cykelløb cycling race
cykelsti bike route

D

dag day
dagens menu price-fixed menu
dal valley
dam pond
dame lady
Danmark Denmark
dans n dance
dansk Danish (language, nationality)
dansker Danish (person)
dejlig delicious
del part
delikatesseforretning delicatessen
deltage attend
deltid part-time
denim denim
deodorant deodorant
der there
desinficeringsmiddel disinfectant

dessert dessert
diabetiker diabetic
diamant diamond
diarré diarrhea
dias slide (photo)
diesel diesel
direkte direct
direktør manager
disk counter
diskotek dance club
dobbeltseng double bed
dobbeltværelse double room
dollar dollar (U.S.)
drej til turn (change direction)
dreng boy
drikkevare n drink
dryppe drip
dråbe drop (liquid)
dukke doll
dusin dozen
dyb deep
dyr adj expensive; n animal
dyrlæge veterinarian
dæk deck (ship)
dårlig bad
dåse can [tin BE]
dåseåbner can [tin BE] opener

E

e-billet e-ticket
e-billet check-in e-ticket check-in
efter after
efterlade v leave (behind)
eftermiddag afternoon
eftermiddagsforestilling matinée
efternavn surname
ekspres express

ekstra extra
elastik n elastic
elektricitet electricity
elektrisk electric
elektronisk electronic
elevator elevator [lift BE]
eller or
elske v love
e-mail e-mail
e-mail-adresse e-mail address
emalje enamel
en a (with common nouns)
en gang once
en masse lot (a lot)
en smule little (amount)
endnu yet
eng meadow
engelsk English (language)
England England
englænder English (person)
enke widow (male)
enkemand widow (female)
enkeltbillet one-way [single BE] ticket
enkeltværelse single room
entré entrance fee
et a (with neuter nouns)
et par stykker few
etage floor
etiket label
eurocheck eurocheque
Europa Europe
Europæiske Fæl-lesskab European Union

F

fabrik factory
faktura invoice
familie family
fantastisk flot stunning
fare danger
faret vild lost
farlig dangerous
farve color
farveblyant crayon
farvel goodbye
farvning dye
fast menu set menu
fax fax
faxnummer fax number
feber fever
fejltagelse mistake
ferie vacation
fest party (social gathering)
fil file (for nails)
film movie [film BE]
filter filter
finde find
finger finger
firkantet square (shape)
fiskekort n permit (fishing)
fiskeri fishing
fjernsyn TV
flaske bottle
flaskegas butane gas
flip collar
flod river; high tide
flonel flannel
fly airplane; flight
flytte v move
fod foot
fodbold soccer [football BE]
fodboldkamp soccer [football BE] match
fodgænger pedestrian
for for

for meget too much
for varm overheated (engine)
forbindelse connection (transportation, internet)
forbløffende amazing
forbudt forbidden
forældre parents
færdig ready
færge ferry
fødsel birth
fødselsdag birthday
født born
føle feel (physical state)
følge follow
føntørre blow-dry
før before (time)
førerhund guide dog
få motorstop breakdown (car)
få ned bring down
få pengene tilbage *v* refund
få udbetalt withdraw (banking)

G

gade street
gadekort street map
gaffel fork
galleri gallery
gamle bydel old town
gammel old
gang *n* time (recurrent occasion)
gangsti trail
garage garage
gardin curtain
gave gift; present
gavebutik gift shop
gaze gauze
gebyr *n* charge
gemme *v* save

genbrugsbutik second-hand shop
genere bother
gennem through
gennemsnitlig average
gentage *v* repeat
gift *adj* married; *n* poison
give give
give adgang for admitted
glad happy
glas glass; jar (container)
glemme forget
god good
godaften good evening
goddag good afternoon
godmorgen good morning
godnat good night
godt fine (OK); well
golfbane golf course
golfkølle golf club
golfturnering golf tournament
grad degree (temperature)
gram gram
grammatik grammar
gravid pregnant
gravsted tomb
grim ugly
grine laugh
gruppe group
gryde pot
grøn green
grønthandler produce store (greengrocer's BE)
grå gray
guide *n* guide
gul yellow
guld gold
guldsmed jeweler

gummi rubber (material)
gummisko sneaker
gynækolog gynecologist
gøre ondt hurt
gøre rent *v* clean
gå ud go out
gå væk go away
gåtur *n* walk

H

hals neck; throat
halskæde necklace
hammer hammer
handicappet disabled
handske glove
hare hare
haste urgent
hat hat
hav sea
have garden
havn harbor; port
hej hello; hi
hele whole
helgengrav shrine
helligdag holiday (public)
helsekostforretning health food store
hente *v* pick up (go get)
her here
herrefrisør barber
hilsen greeting
hilsner regards
himmel sky
historie history
hittegodskontor lost and found (lost property office BE)
hjelm helmet
hjem home
hjemmesko slipper
hjerte heart
hjerteanfald heart attack

hjertebanken palpitations
hjul wheel
hjælp assistance; help
hjælp på vejen roadside assistance
hjørne corner
hold team
hospital hospital
hoste *n* cough
hotel hotel
hotelfortegnelse hotel directory
hoved head
hovedpine headache
hovedpinepille aspirin
hovedtelefon headphones
hr. Mr.
hud skin
hukommelseskort memory card
hul hole
hule cave
hund dog
hurtig *adj* fast; quick
hus house
husholdningsartikel household item
hvad what
hvem who
hver each; every
hvid white
hvilken which
hvis if
hvor where
hvor langt how far
hvor længe how long
hvor mange how many
hvor meget how much
hvor som helst anywhere
hvordan how
hvorfor why
hvornår when

hygiejnebind sanitary napkin [pad BE]
hylde shelf
hyttesko loafers
hæfteklamme staple
hængekøje hammock
hæve swell
hævelse swelling
hævet swollen
høfeber hay fever
høj high; loud (volume)
høj stol highchair
højhalset turtleneck
høre på listen
hørehæmmet hearing impaired
hånd hand
håndcreme hand cream
håndklæde towel
håndlavet handmade
håndtaske purse [handbag BE]
hår hair
hårbørste hairbrush
hård hard
hårlak hairspray
hårtørrer hair dryer

I

i aften tonight
i dag today
i går yesterday
i løbet af during
i morgen tomorrow
i nærheden nearby
i stykker broken
iberegne include
id-kort identification (card)
igen again
ikke not
ikke noget nothing
ikke-ryger non-smoking
imponerende impressive

importeret imported
indbyde v invite
indbydelse invitation
indeholde contain
indendørs indoor
indenfor inside
indenrigs domestic (airport terminal)
indenrigsfly domestic flight
indgang entrance
indkøb shopping
indkøbscenter shopping area
indkøbsvogn cart
indløse v cash
indre by downtown area
indskrivning registration
indskud n deposit (bank)
indsprøjtning injection
indtaste v enter
indtil until
influenza flu
information information
informationsluge information desk
ingen none
insekt bug
insektbid insect bite
insekt-spray insect repellent
instant messenger instant messenger
interessant interesting
interesseret interested
international international (airport terminal)
internet internet
internetcafé internet cafe
investering investment
Irland Ireland

irlænder Irish
isenkræmmer hardware store
iskoldt icy (weather)

J

ja yes
jagt hunting
jakke jacket
jazz jazz
jeg I
jernbanestation train [railway BE] station
jetski jet ski
jod iodine

K

kahyt cabin (ship)
kalender calendar
kam comb
kamera camera
kamp n match (sport)
kampplads battleground
kan v can (be able to)
kapel chapel
karaffel carafe
karton carton (of cigarettes)
kasino casino
kasket cap
kasse cash desk; cashier
kasserolle saucepan
kedelig boring
kemisk toilet chemical toilet
keramik ceramics
ketsjer racket (sport)
kikkert binoculars
kilde n spring (water)
kilogram kilogram
kilometer kilometer
kilometerpenge mileage

kirke church
kirkegård cemetery
kirtel gland
kjole n dress
klage complaint
klapseng cot
klapvogn stroller [pushchair BE]
klassisk classical
klimaanlæg air conditioning
klipning haircut
klister paste (glue)
klokken o'clock
knallert moped
knap button
kniv knife
knogle bone
knæ knee
kobber copper
koble sig fra v disconnect (computer)
koble sig på v connect (computer)
kollega colleague
komme come
komme med join
komme til get (find)
komme til skade injure
komme tilbage return (give back)
kommission commission (fee)
kompas compass
koncert concert
koncertsal concert hall
konditori pastry shop
kondom condom
kone wife
konferencesal convention hall
konsulat consulate
kontaktlinse contact lens

konto account
kontor office
kontrakt contract
kontrol control
konvolut envelope
kop cup
kort card; map; *adj* short
kortspil card game
kortsynet near-sighted [short-sighted BE]
kost diet
kost broom
kramme *v* hug
krampe cramps
kranbil tow truck
kravlegård playpen
kredit credit
kreditkort credit card
kro inn
krone crown (Danish currency)
krop body
krus *n* mug (cup)
krystal crystal
kuffert suitcase
kuglepen pen
kun only
kunne able
kunst art
kunstgalleri art gallery
kunsthåndværk handicrafts
kupé compartment (train)
kurv basket
kvalitet quality
kvalme nausea
kvarter district (of town)
kvinde woman
kvindelig tjener waitress
kvittering receipt
kvæstelse injury
kysse *v* kiss

kæbe jaw
kæreste boyfriend; girlfriend
køb *n* purchase
købe buy
køje berth
køkken cuisine
køkkenchef chef
køkkenfaciliteter cooking facilities
køleskab refrigerator
kølle mallet
køn attractive; pretty
køn rute scenic route
køre drive
køre tilbage go back
kørekort driver's license
køreplan schedule [timetable BE]
kørestol wheelchair
køresyge travel sickness

L

laktoseintolerant lactose intolerant
lampe lamp
land country
landsby village
landskab landscape; scenery
lange long
langrend cross-country skiing
langsom slow
langsynet far-sighted [long-sighted BE]
langt far
lappe patch
lav low
led *n* joint (anatomy)
ledig vacant
ledigt free
ledigt værelse vacancy
legeplads playground

legetøj toy
legetøjsforretning toy store
leje *v* rent [hire BE]
lejlighed apartment [flat BE]
let light (weight)
levere deliver
levering delivery
ligeud straight ahead
liggestol deck chair
lighter lighter
lille small
lim glue
liter liter
livredder life guard (beach)
log ind login
logge af log off
logge på log on
lokal extension (phone); local
lomme pocket
lommelygte flashlight
lommetørklæde handkerchief
loppemarked flea market
lotion lotion
lufthavn airport
luftmadras air mattress
luftpost airmail
lukke *v* close
lunge lung
lungebetændelse pneumonia
lydguide audio guide
lygte lantern
lykke luck
lyn lightning
lynlås zipper
lys light (color)
lyserød pink
lystspil comedy

læbe lip
læbestift lipstick
læder leather
læge doctor
lægekonsultation doctor's office [surgery BE]
lærred linen
lår thigh

M

mad food
made *v* feed
madforgiftning food poisoning
madkurv picnic basket
madras mattress
maleri painting
maling *n* paint
manchetknap cufflink
mand husband; man
mange many
mangle *v* miss (lacking)
manicure manicure
mark field
marked market
marskandiser second-hand shop
massage massage
mave stomach
mavepine stomachache
med with
medbragt mad picnic
medicin medicine (drug)
meget much; very
mejeri dairy
mekaniker mechanic
mellem between
mellemmåltid snack
men but
menstruation period (menstrual)
menu menu
mere more

messe fair (event); mass (religious service)
meter meter
metro subway [underground BE]
metrostation subway [underground BE] station
middag dinner; noon
midlertidig temporary
midnat midnight
midten middle
mindesmærke memorial
mindre less
mindst at least
minut minute
miste lose
mobiltelefon cell [mobile BE] phone
mod against; toward
modtageren betaler call collect [reverse the charges BE]
moms sales tax [value-added tax BE]
monument monument
moppe n mop
morgen morning
morgenmad breakfast
morgenvækning wake-up call
moské mosque
motel motel
motionscenter gym
motorbåd motorboat
motorcykel motorcycle
motorvej highway [motorway BE]
mund mouth
mundvand mouthwash
mur wall
museum museum
musical musical

musik music
muskel muscle
myggenet mosquito net
mængde quantity
møbel furniture
mødelokale conference room
mødes meet
mønster pattern
mønt coin
møntvaskeri laundromat [launderette BE]
mørk dark
må may (can)
målekrus measuring cup
måleske measuring spoon
måltid meal
måne moon
måned month
måske perhaps
måtte must (have to)

N

narkose anesthetic
nat night
nationalitet nationality
naturlig natural
navn name
ned down
nedenunder below
nederdel skirt
negl nail (body)
neglefil nail file
negleklipper nail clippers
neglesalon nail salon
nej no
nem easy
nerve nerve
nogen any; anyone; someone; some
noget anything; some;

something
nogle some
nok enough
nord north
normal adj normal
normalt adv usually
notesbog notebook
nu now
nummer number
ny new
nyre kidney
nær near
næse nose
næste next
nødhjælpskasse first-aid kit
nødstilfælde emergency
nødudgang emergency exit
nødvendig required
nøgle key
nøglekort key card
nål n pin (brooch); needle

O

objektiv lens (camera)
og and
også also; too
omkring around (approximately)
omkørsel detour (traffic)
område region
ondt i halsen sore throat
ondt i ørerne earache
op up
opera opera; opera house
operation operation
oplukker bottle opener
opsparingskonto savings account
optaget busy; occupied
optiker optician

opvarme v heat
opvaskemaskine dishwasher
opvaskemiddel detergent
orange orange (color)
ord word
ordbog dictionary
orkester orchestra
oval oval
ovenpå above; upstairs
overfald n attack; mugging
overfart crossing (maritime)
overfor opposite
overførsel transfer (money wire)
overskud n profit
overskæg moustache
overslag n estimate
oversætte translate
overtjener head waiter
ovn stove
oxygenbehandling oxygen treatment

P

pakke package [parcel BE]
papir paper
papirhandel stationery store
papirhåndklæde paper towel
papirslommetørklæde tissue
par pair
paraply umbrella
parfume perfume
park n park
parkering parking
parkeringskælder parking garage

parkeringsplads parking lot [car park BE]
parkeringsskive parking disc
parkometer parking meter
pas passport
pasfoto passport photo
paskontrol passport control
passe *v* fit
patient patient
pc computer
pedicure pedicure
pege *v* point
pen pen
penge money
pengeautomat ATM
penicillin penicillin
pensionat guesthouse
pensioneret retired
pensionist senior citizen
per dag per day
per person per person
per time per hour
per uge per week
perle pearl
perron platform (station)
person person
personale staff
personlig personal
petit petite
pibe pipe
pige girl
pille pill; tablet (medical)
pincet tweezers
pinkode PIN
plads seat
pladsreserveringen reservations office
planetarium planetarium
plaster *n* bandage

[plaster BE]
plastic plastic
plasticpose plastic bag
plastikfolie plastic wrap
platin platinum
plet stain
plombe filling (tooth)
pløk peg (tent)
politi police
politianmeldelse police report
politistation police station
porcelæn porcelain
portier porter
portion portion
porto postage
post *n* mail [post BE]
postanvisning money order
poste restante general delivery
posthus post office
postkasse mailbox [postbox BE]
postkort postcard
pottemageri pottery
praktiserende læge doctor [general practitioner BE]
presse press (iron)
pris price
privat private
procentsats percentage
program program (of events)
proptrækker corkscrew
protese denture
præsentation introduction (social)
præsentere introduce
præventivmiddel contraceptive
prøverum fitting room

pudder powder
pude pillow
pumpe pump
pund pound (British currency, weight)
punktering puncture
pyjamas pajamas
pære light bulb
på on
på landet countryside
pålidelig reliable

R

rabat discount
rabatkort booklet (of tickets)
radio radio
rav amber
reb rope
recept prescription
reception reception
receptionist receptionist
redningsbælte life preserver
redningsbåd life boat
redningsvest life jacket
regnemaskine calculator
regnfrakke raincoat
regning check [bill BE] (restaurant)
regnvejr rain
rejse journey; travel; trip
rejsebureau travel agency
rejsecheck traveler's check [cheque BE]
rejsefører guidebook
rejsefører travel guide
rektangulær rectangular
religion religion
ren clean; pure
rensecreme cleansing

cream
renseri dry cleaner
rente interest (finance)
reparation *n* repair
reparere *v* fix; mend
reservation reservation
reserveret reserved
rest *n* rest
restaurant restaurant
ret dish (food item)
retsbygning court house
returbillet round-trip [return BE] ticket
returnere return (come back)
reumatisme rheumatism
ribben rib
ridning horseback riding
rigtigt right (correct)
ring ring (jewelry)
ringeklokke bell (electric)
rive i stykker *v* tear
robåd rowboat
rolig calm
romantisk romantic
roomservice room service
rubin ruby
rullegardin blind (window)
rulletrappe escalator
rumtemperatur room temperature
rund round
runde round (golf)
rundt om around (the corner)
rundtur sightseeing tour
rustfrit stål stainless steel
rute route
ryg back

ryge smoke
rygrad spine
rygsæk backpack
rød red
røntgenfotografere
X-ray
røre v touch
rådhus town hall

S

safir sapphire
saks scissors
sal hall (room)
saldo balance (finance)
salg n sale
samme same
sand sand
sandal sandal
sang song
satin satin
sauna sauna
scooter scooter
se v look
seddel bill (bank note)
sejlbåd sailboat
sekund second
sele seat belt
sende send
senere later
seng bed
sent late (time)
separeret separated
(relationship)
servere serve (meal)
service på værelset
room service
serviet napkin
seværdighed point of
interest
shampoo shampoo
side side
siden since
sidst last
sige tell

sightseeing sightseeing
sikker adj safe
sikkerhedsnål safety
pin
silke silk
skaffe provide
skak chess
skakspil chess set
skarp sharp (pain)
skat tax
ske spoon
skib n ship
skilt notice (sign)
skive n slice
skjorte shirt
sko shoe
skodde shutter (window)
skoforretning shoe
store
skole school
Skotland Scotland
skov forest
skovl n shovel
skrald garbage (rub-
bish BE)
skrive write
skrive recept på
prescribe
skruetrækker
screwdriver
skrædder tailor
skubbe v push
skulder shoulder
skulle have (must)
skulptur sculpture
sky cloud
skæg beard
skøjte v skate
skøjtebane skating rink
skønhedssalon beauty
salon
slags sort (kind)
slagter butcher
slebet glas cut glass

slette v clear
slips tie
slipseklemme tie clip
slot palace
sluge swallow
slutning end
smal narrow
smaragd emerald
smerte ache; pain
smerter i brystet
chest pain
smerter i ryggen
backache
smertestillende
middel analgesic;
painkiller
sminke n make-up
smitsom contagious
smuk beautiful
snackbar snack bar
snart soon
snevejr snow
snitsår n cut (wound)
snor string
snorkeludstyr snorke-
ling equipment
sokke sock
sol sun
solbriller sunglasses
solcreme sun-tan lotion
solforbrænding sunburn
solid sturdy
solstik sunstroke
sort black
souvenir souvenir
souvenirbutik souvenir
shop
sove v sleep
sovepille sleeping pill
sovepose sleeping bag
sovevogn sleeping car
spa spa
spand bucket; pail
spatel spatula

specialist specialist
specialitet speciality
spejl mirror
spil game
spillehal arcade
spillekort playing card
spise eat
spiseolie oil
spisesalen dining room
spisevogn dining car
spor track (train)
sport sport
sportsforretning sport-
ing goods store
sporvogn tram
springvand fountain
spænding voltage
spørgsmål n question
stadium stadium
stave v spell
stearinlys candle
sted n place
stegepande frying pan
stel frame (glasses)
sterlingsølv sterling
silver
sti path
stige af get off
stik plug (electric)
stik n sting
stikkontakt electrical
outlet
stikpille suppository
stille quiet
stilling occupation
stjerne star
stjæle steal
stof cloth; fabric;
material
stol chair
stoppet blocked
stor big; large
stor størrelse plus-size

storartet great (excellent)

Storbritannien Great Britain

stormagasin department store

strand beach

strikvarer knitwear

strygejern iron (clothing)

strøm current (ocean)

strømpe stockings

strømpebukser panty hose

studere study

studerende student

studsning trim

stuepige maid

stykke piece; play (theater)

stærk strong

stævnemøde date (appointment)

støjende noisy

størrelse size

støvle boot

støvsuger vacuum cleaner

stå op get up

sulten hungry

supermarked supermarket

sut pacifier [dummy BE] (baby's)

sutteflaske baby bottle

svamp sponge

svar answer

svimmel dizzy

svimmingpool pool

svuppert plunger

svær difficult

svømme v swim

svømmebassin pool

svømning swimming

sweater sweater

sweatshirt sweatshirt

sy sew

syd south

syg ill [BE]

sygdom disease; illness

sygeforsikring health insurance

sygeplejerske nurse

symbol symbol

syn eyesight

synagoge synagogue

synge sing

synshæmmet visually impaired

syntetisk synthetic

system system

sæbe soap

sæde ved midtergangen aisle seat

sælge sell

særlig special

sæson season

sætning sentence

sætte put

sætte sig sit down

sø lake

sød sweet

sølv silver

sølvtøj silverware

så then

sår wound

T

tab loss

tage take

tage imod v accept

tage med bring; to go [take away BE]

tage mål af measure

tage tøjet af undress

taget taken (occupied)

tak thank you

takke thank

tale v speak

tallerken plate

tampon tampon

tand tooth

tandbørste toothbrush

tandlæge dentist

tandpasta toothpaste

tandpine toothache

tarm bowel

taske case (camera)

taske bag (purse)

taxa taxi

taxaholdeplads taxi stand [rank BE]

teater theater

tegnebog wallet

telefon n telephone

telefonbog telephone directory

telefonboks telephone booth

telefonist operator

telefonkort phone card

telefonnummer telephone number

telt tent

teltpløk tent peg

teltstang tent pole

teltunderlag groundsheet

tempel temple

temperatur temperature

tennisbane tennis court

tenniskamp tennis match

tennisketsjer tennis racket

terminal terminal

termometer thermometer

terrasse terrace

teske teaspoon

tid n time

tidligt early

til to

til lykke congratulations

til tiden on time

til venstre left

tilbehør accessory

tillæg n supplement

time hour (time)

tinlegering pewter

tjekke ud v check out

tjener waiter

tobak tobacco

tobakshandler tobacconist

tog train

togkort subway [underground BE] map

toilet restroom [toilet BE]

toiletartikel toiletry

toiletpapir toilet paper

told customs; duty

toldangivelsesformular customs declaration form

toldfri butik duty-free shop

toldfri varer duty-free goods

tolk interpreter

tom empty

tommelfinger thumb

torden thunder

tordenvejr thunderstorm

trafiklys traffic light

transportabel portable

trappe stairs

travlt hurry

trist gloomy

tro think (believe)

tryk pressure

træ tree

trække v pull

trække vejret breathe

trækul charcoal

træt tired
tråd thread
trådløs wireless
T-shirt T-shirt
tube tube
tung heavy
tunge tongue
tur tour
turistkontor tourist
  office
tynd thin
tyv thief
tyveri robbery
tyveri theft
tæppe blanket
tøj clothing
tøjbutik clothing store
tør dry
tørklæde scarf
tørstig thirsty
tå toe
tåge fog
tårn tower

U

uden without
udenfor outside
udenlandsk foreign
udenrigsfly interna-
  tional flight
udflugt excursion
udfylde fill in (form)
udgang n exit
udgift expense
udkigspost n overlook
udlejning rental
udlejningsbil rental car
udsalg sale (bargains)
udsigt view (panorama)
udskrive v print (document)
udslet rash
udsolgt out of stock;
  sold out

udspecificeret regning
  itemized bill
udstilling exhibition
udstillingsmontre
  display case
udstyr appliance;
  equipment
udtale pronunciation
udtryk expression
uge week
uld wool
ulykke accident
under under
underbukser
  underpants
underkop saucer
underlig strange
underrette notify
underskrift signature
underskrive sign
undersøgelse check-up
  (medical)
undertrøje undershirt
undervisning lesson
undskylde v excuse
ung young
universitet university
ur clock; watch
USA United States
uskyldig innocent

V

vaccinere vaccinate
valuta currency
vand water
vandfald waterfall
vandhane faucet
vandrehjem youth
  hostel
vandski waterski
vandtæt waterproof
vare article (merchan-
  dise)
varm hot; warm

  (temperature)
varme heat [heating BE]
vaske i hånden hand
  washable
vaske v wash
vaskemaskine washing
  machine
vaskeri laundry service
vaskerum laundry
  facilities
vaskesuger plunger
vasketøj laundry
ved at
ved siden af next to
vedhæng pendant
vegetar vegetarian
vej road; way
vejangivelse direction
vejkort road map
vejkryds crossroads;
  intersection
vejr weather
vejrudsigt weather
  forecast
vejskilt road sign
vekselkontor currency
  exchange office
vekselkurs exchange
  rate
veksle v exchange
  (money)
ven friend
vending phrase
vene vein
vente v expect; wait
venteværelse waiting
  room
ventilator fan
vest west
v-hals v-neck
vi we
vide know
videokamera video
  camera

vigtig important
vil gerne like
ville have want
vind wind
vindue window
vinduessæde window
  seat
vinhandel liquor store
  [off-licence BE]
vinliste wine list
violet purple
virke v work
virkelig hyggelig
  wonderful
virker ikke out of order
vis certain
vise vej til v direct
  (someone)
visitkort business card
viskelæder eraser
voldtægt n rape
volleyballkamp vol-
  leyball game
væddeløb race
væddeløbsbane race
  track
væk away
vække wake
vækkeur alarm clock
vælg choice
vær venlig please
værdi value
være be
værelse room (hotel)
værelsesbestilling hotel
  reservation
værelsesnummer room
  number
værktøj tool
værre worse
væske fluid
vådservietter baby
  wipes

W

Wales Wales
weekend weekend
windsurfer windsurfer

Z

zoologisk have zoo

Æ

ædelsten gem
ægte genuine; real
ændre v alter
ærme sleeve
æske box

Ø

øje eye

øjeblik moment
øjendråber eye drops
øjenskygge eye shadow
økonomiklasse
  economy class
øm sore (painful)
ønske v wish
øre ear
øredråber ear drops

ørenring earring
øst east

Å

åben open
åbne v open
år year

INDEX

COPENHAGEN

Ninth edition 2020

Editor: Siobhan Warwicker
Author: Norman Renouf, Fran Parnell
Head of DTP and Pre-Press: Rebeka Davies
Managing Editor: Carine Tracanelli
Picture Editor: Aude Vauconsant
Layout: Agnieszka Bylica
Cartography Update: Carte
Update Production: Apa Digital
Photography Credits: akg-images 17,18; Anders Kjærbye/Copenhagen Media Center 93; Astrid Maria Rasmussen/Copenhagen Media Center 95; Büro Jantzen/Copenhagen Media Center 104; Cees van Roeden/Copenhagen Media Center 40; Corbis 5M; Daniel Rasmussen/Copenhagen Media Center 21, 24; David Hall/Apa Publications 6L; Dianne Pavletich/Copenhagen Media Center 1; Ditte Isager/Copenhagen Media Center 101; Glyptoteket/Copenhagen Media Center 47; iStock 5TC, 11, 26, 63, 64, 94; Krause & Johansen 86; Martin Heiberg/Copenhagen Media Center 81; Morten Jerichau/Copenhagen Media Center 48, 66; Rasmus Flindt Pedersen/Copenhagen Media Center 6R; Rudy Hemmingsen/Apa Publications 4TC, 4MC, 4ML, 4TL, 5T, 5M, 13, 28, 30, 33, 34, 36, 38, 43, 45, 50, 53, 55, 56, 58, 60, 61, 65, 69, 71, 73, 74, 75, 76, 78, 85, 88, 90; Shutterstock 5MC, 7TL; Thomas Høyrup Christensen/Copenhagen Media Center 5MC; Thomas Ibsen/Copenhagen Media Center 97; Ty Stange/Copenhagen Media Center 7R, 84; Wonderful Copenhagen; 14, 82, 99, 102
Cover Picture: Shutterstock

Distribution
UK, Ireland and Europe: Apa Publications (UK) Ltd; sales@insightguides.com
United States and Canada: Ingram Publisher Services; ips@ingramcontent.com

Australia and New Zealand: Woodslane; info@woodslane.com.au
Southeast Asia: Apa Publications (SN) Pte; singaporeoffice@insightguides.com
Worldwide: Apa Publications (UK) Ltd; sales@insightguides.com

Special Sales, Content Licensing and CoPublishing
Insight Guides can be purchased in bulk quantities at discounted prices. We can create special editions, personalised jackets and corporate imprints tailored to your needs. sales@insightguides.com; www.insightguides.biz

Contact us
Every effort has been made to provide accurate information in this publication, but changes are inevitable. The publisher cannot be responsible for any resulting loss, inconvenience or injury. We would appreciate it if readers would call our attention to any errors or outdated information. We also welcome your suggestions; please contact us at: berlitz@apaguide.co.uk
www.insightguides.com/berlitz

Copenhagen Metro

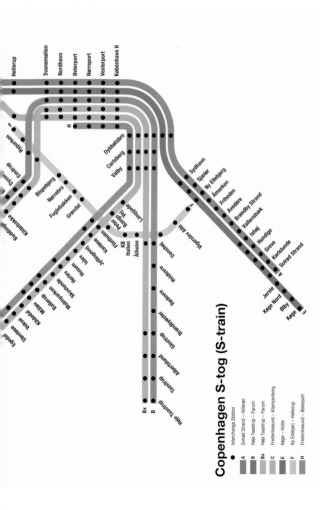

Copenhagen S-tog (S-train)

● Interchange Station

A	Solrød Strand – Hillerød
B	Høje Taastrup – Farum
Bx	Høje Taastrup – Farum
C	Frederikssund – Klampenborg
E	Køge – Holte
F	Ny Ellebjerg – Hellerup
H	Frederikssund – Østerport

Berlitz®

speaking your language

phrase book & dictionary
phrase book & CD

Available in: Arabic, Brazilian Portuguese*, Burmese*, Cantonese
Chinese, Croatian, Czech*, Danish*, Dutch, English, Filipino, Finnish*, French,
German, Greek, Hebrew*, Hindi*, Hungarian*, Indonesian, Italian, Japanese,
Korean, Latin American Spanish, Malay, Mandarin Chinese, Mexican Spanish,
Norwegian, Polish, Portuguese, Romanian*, Russian, Spanish, Swedish, Thai,
Turkish, Vietnamese
*Book only